FENG SHUI
IN YOUR GARDEN

FENG SHUI
IN YOUR GARDEN

How to Create Harmony in Your Garden

RONI JAY

RICHARD CRAZE • CONSULTANT

A GODSFIELD BOOK

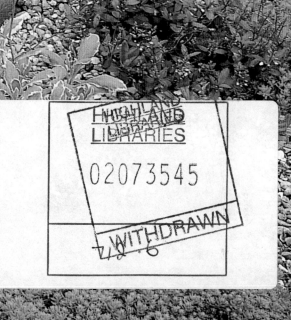

First published in Great Britain in 1998
This edition published in 2000
by Godsfield Press Ltd,
a division of David and Charles Ltd,
Laurel House, Station Approach, Alresford, Hants
SO24 9JH

10 9 8 7 6 5 4 3 2 1

COPYRIGHT © 1998 GODSFIELD PRESS

Text © 1998 Roni Jay

With thanks to Glen and Tony Eastman for the use of
their photographs on the following pages:
Tony Eastman p32, p34 (*sculpture by Philip Booth*), p69
(*top right*), p73
Glen Eastman p72

Picture research by Jane Moore

Designed for Godsfield Press by
The Bridgewater Book Company

ISBN 1-84181-043-6

Printed in Hong Kong

Introduction

Feng shui is *the ancient Chinese art of harmonizing your surroundings to influence your health, success, and happiness. The words feng shui (pronounced "fung shoy" or "fung shway") mean "wind" and "water"; the cosmic energy, which the Chinese believe is present in everything, flows like wind and like water. The art lies in influencing the flow of energy to maximize the good fortune it imparts. Many books tell you how you can apply these principles in your home or office; this book concentrates on how to apply them in your garden.*

There are two ways of achieving good feng shui, both of which are traditionally used in conjunction with each other. The first is to choose your surroundings according to their feng shui, making sure that they are naturally propitious for you. However, since things are rarely perfect, the second approach to feng shui is geared toward making changes to improve those aspects that are not as lucky as they might be.

CREATING PERFECT FENG SHUI

Feng Shui in the Garden will show you how to create perfect feng shui in your garden. If you are looking for a new house, it will help you evaluate the property to see whether it is suitable. If you are designing a garden, you can use the techniques in this book to make sure you create one that gives you what you want. If you already have an established garden, this book is full of techniques and ideas for making changes that will improve its feng shui.

Adapting the feng shui of your garden to maximize the benefits you derive from it doesn't have to mean huge, expensive upheaval. Sometimes tiny changes can make a huge difference to the flow of energy through the garden. It may help to change the layout of paths and flowerbeds, or you may simply need to cut back an overly large shrub, or add a

The colors of the flowers in a border can improve the feng shui of the garden. In this traditional English border, bright colors have instinctively been chosen to liven up the flow of energy.

birdbath, or change the color of the flowers in a particular section of the garden. You can often make a substantial difference with simple techniques such as adding an ornament or a statue, repainting a lawn chair, or opening up an overgrown area.

We all want something different from our garden. If you want your garden to provide what you need – whether it is a space for meditation, a safe play area for your children, a place to entertain friends or a productive vegetable garden – feng shui will help you achieve it.

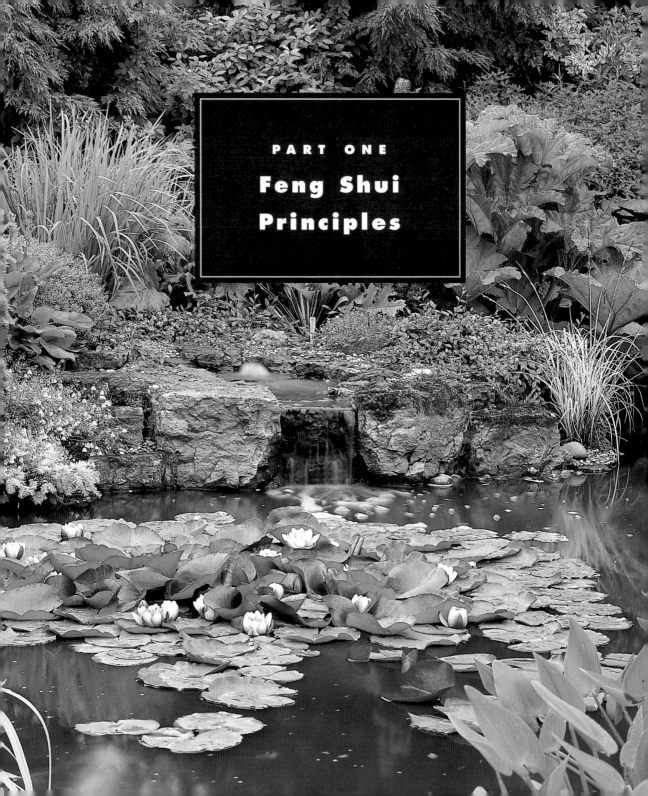

PART ONE
Feng Shui
Principles

Principles of Feng Shui

ACCORDING TO *Chinese tradition, everything in the world contains cosmic energy, known as ch'i. Ch'i needs to flow smoothly and freely through its surroundings in order to create harmony. But its movement can be disrupted if it is blocked, trapped in a dead end, funneled through tunnel-like paths and passages, or forced to cascade over obstacles or through openings. This in turn causes disharmony in your life. Ch'i is encouraged or deterred by certain shapes, colors, sounds, and movement, and the art of feng shui is all about guiding the movement of ch'i to insure an even, balanced flow.*

To understand feng shui properly, you need to understand the concept of yin and yang, which is central to Taoism, the ancient religion of China. According to Taoism, everything in the universe contains ch'i, the cosmic life force; and ch'i itself is mixed from two forms of energy: yin and yang. Yin energy is sometimes known as the feminine principle, and yang energy as the masculine principle. But yin and yang energy are more subtle than this. Yang energy is about elements such as openness, light, heat, summer, and daytime. It represents the spirit. Yin energy, on the other hand, is about shadows, darkness, coldness, winter, nighttime, and other related aspects. It represents matter.

Everything contains either yin or yang ch'i. Foods, parts of the body, plants

---

YANG

Spirit, Male, Day, Light, Sun, Summer, Dry, Hard, Heat, Creative, Active, Positive, Sky, Heaven, South, Outer

YIN

Matter, Female, Night, Dark, Shade, Winter, Wet, Soft, Cold, Receptive, Passive, Negative, Earth, Creation, North, Inner,

---

– each is either yin or yang. But since ch'i is made of both yin and yang, it is impossible for anything to be wholly one or the other – it must always be balanced by a little of its counterpart. Yin and yang are not opposites; they are complementary to

each other. This is why the yin/yang symbol looks as it does: the white yang part has a dot of black yin in it, and the black yin half of the symbol contains a white dot of yang.

When you adapt your surroundings to improve their feng shui, one of the things you must do is ensure that the ch'i flowing through them is made up of an equal balance of yin and yang energies. Too much dark yin energy can create a

heavy, sleepy effect, and too much yang energy can lead to too much stimulation and unpredictability.

WHERE DOES THE CH'I COME FROM?

The ch'i that flows around your garden (or your house, your office, or anywhere else) has to come from somewhere. It arrives in your garden from all around its borders, coming in through gateways, through gaps in fences, over walls, and under hedges. And when it arrives, it is already imbued with its own type of energy depending on the direction from which it has arrived.

Ch'i from the north is very different from ch'i that comes from the south. Western ch'i and eastern ch'i are different again. And before you can hope to improve the feng shui of your garden, you have to know what kind of ch'i you are dealing with. According to Chinese tradition, each of the four main compass directions is governed by its own animal; these animals symbolize the energy that flows from their part of the compass.

right: *Adding a piece of sculpture in your garden can have tremendous effect. A well-placed work can be used to steady the flow of ch'i as well as having a pleasing visual impact.*

THE FOUR MAIN COMPASS DIRECTIONS

SOUTH: This is the direction of the Red Phoenix. The ch'i flowing from here is very propitious – south is generally believed to be the best direction for a house or garden to face. Ch'i from the south is bright, lucky, happy, and full of energy. However, it is possible to have too much of a good thing, and if your garden is very open to the south and the ch'i floods in from this direction, it can become overpowering. It is very yang ch'i and may need to be calmed down a little, especially if you like to use your garden for peaceful activities such as meditation or winding down at the end of a busy day. (We will look at techniques for calming down overpowering ch'i later on.)

NORTH: The Black Tortoise governs the north and it brings nurturing yin ch'i. This is excellent for a part of the garden where children play because it is very caring and protective. However, it can become heavy and sleepy unless you introduce lighter, more yang energy to counterbalance it.

WEST: This is the area of the White Tiger, which brings an unpredictable, sometimes dangerous energy with it. You need to prevent too much ch'i entering your garden from that direction. However, it can be a useful energy to encourage in small doses since it can be ideal for pepping up dead areas where the ch'i is prone to stagnate.

EAST: The direction of the Green Dragon. Ch'i from the east is kind and wise, and encourages growth. In large doses, however, it can result in parts of your garden being too fecund and hence becoming overgrown.

THE SECONDARY COMPASS POINTS

The four intermediate compass directions also bring their own kind of ch'i, which can manifest itself in both positive and negative ways:

SOUTHWEST: This ch'i is soothing and gentle, combining the expansiveness of the Phoenix with the wisdom of the Dragon. However, if it becomes too strong it can overpower the yin energy of the garden.

SOUTHEAST: This is creative and imaginative energy, but when too much of it is present it can become overproductive and provoking, making it hard to relax peacefully in the garden.

NORTHWEST: This ch'i is open and still, bringing peace and tranquility when the

16

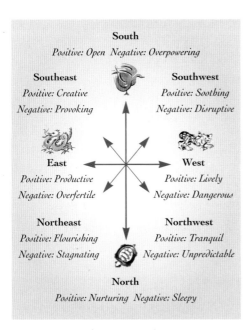

South
Positive: Open Negative: Overpowering

Southeast
Positive: Creative
Negative: Provoking

Southwest
Positive: Soothing
Negative: Disruptive

East
Positive: Productive
Negative: Overfertile

West
Positive: Lively
Negative: Dangerous

Northeast
Positive: Flourishing
Negative: Stagnating

Northwest
Positive: Tranquil
Negative: Unpredictable

North
Positive: Nurturing Negative: Sleepy

Figure 1: The eight compass points
The Chinese always show south at the top of their feng shui compasses and charts, since south is the direction from which the most positive and propitious ch'i flows.

sleepy Tortoise and the changeable Tiger are in balance. But there is a risk of the balance becoming tipped in favor of the Tiger, resulting in unpredictable energy.

NORTHEAST: This combines the Dragon's growth and productivity with the nurturing energy of the Tortoise, creating an ideal environment for plants to flourish. The risk is that the Tortoise's energy will become dominant and the ch'i will begin to stagnate.

THE EIGHT AREAS

Your garden, or any other property where you are studying the feng shui, is divided into eight areas for the purposes of assessing its feng shui. Each of these eight areas influences a different aspect of your life, such as your relationships or your health. Once you know which part of your own garden falls into each of these eight areas, you can begin to apply the principles of feng shui. You can examine each part of the garden in turn, establish what kind of ch'i it is receiving, and assess this in terms of the aspect of your life that it influences. For example, you may find that part of your garden is full of unpredictable ch'i from the west. If this is the area of your garden that influences your health, you may well be prone to bouts of sudden illness. Or perhaps a high hedge is blocking the beneficial ch'i which should flow in from the south; this could lead to stagnation in the part of your life influenced by the south part of your garden.

We will discuss later how to establish which part of your garden influences each of the eight areas of your life, and which activities best suit each part of the garden. We will also look at what you can do to put right any problem areas.

Feng Shui in the Garden

A**S WE SHALL SEE,** *cosmic energy – or ch'i – flows in and around everything. To be harmonious it must flow smoothly, in gentle curves, without being allowed either to stagnate or to be funneled into moving too fast. You need to guide the ch'i in your garden to create the most harmonious energy flow. This harmony, once you have achieved it, will influence you in return, and you will find your own moods and fortunes will improve as a result.*

BORROWING FROM THE LANDSCAPE

The principles of feng shui are drawn from centuries of observing the natural world and its landscapes. Ch'i can be moved by the wind and weather, and the ancient Chinese were aware of the differing effects of ch'i that blew fast over craggy cliffs, or drifted gently on the breeze over rolling hills, or hung over vast plains, or funneled into steep valleys. They noted these effects and learned to control the flow of ch'i in order to maximize the benefits they could derive from it.

Nowadays feng shui is often applied to buildings and interiors, but the outside world is the original home of feng shui. And the ch'i that flows around your

above: *Without the birdbath to contrast with the foliage this hosta bed would be dull and uninteresting, a place of stagnant energy.*

above: *We all want something different from our garden – feng shui will help your work come to fruition whatever you choose to use your garden for.*

house cannot reach the doors and windows without passing through your garden. So it's the logical place to begin to control and guide the ch'i.

NATURAL GOOD TASTE

There's another reason for paying close attention to the feng shui of your garden. What is the aim of feng shui? To create harmony and balance. And what is a garden for? It's a place where we can be in harmony with the natural world. We may use it for entertaining friends or growing vegetables, but almost all of us value the garden as a place we can sit in peacefully when we need to restore our natural balance.

One of the greatest benefits of creating good feng shui in your garden is that ch'i seems to have very good taste. Any changes you need to make to improve its flow always seem to improve the garden from an esthetic point of view as well. You often find that you add or move something to improve the flow of ch'i, and then you stand back and find yourself thinking, "I much prefer that. Why didn't I think of it before?"

The Direction of Your Garden

*I*N ORDER *to assess and improve the feng shui of your garden, you need to draw up an individual chart for it. This will tell you which areas of your garden correlate with each of the eight aspects of your life that are influenced by feng shui. The main piece of information you need to establish to draw up this chart (or pah kwa, as it is known) is which direction the garden faces. So this is the first thing you need to establish before you can begin.*

When you want to know which way your house faces, it's quite simple – it faces out through the front door. But when it comes to the garden, it can be a little more difficult to recognize which way it faces. However, generally speaking, your garden faces in the direction from which you normally enter it. So if you enter it from the street, and the street is to the south, your garden faces south. If you usually reach your garden through your backdoor, in the northwest of the garden, then the garden faces northwest. If the garden is separate from the house with its own entrance, it faces toward this.

USING YOUR INTUITION

A certain amount of intuition is sometimes called for in establishing the direction of your garden. Although you can apply the techniques of feng shui according to the rules and guidelines set out in this book, a good intuitive sense is always a useful backup in helping you to identify problem areas or to choose the best remedies for correcting a bad flow of ch'i. So you might as well start using your intuition now.

If there is more than one entrance that you regularly use to enter your garden, you will have to decide

FINDING THE DIRECTION

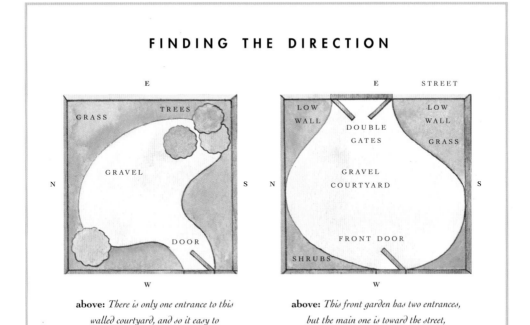

above: *There is only one entrance to this walled courtyard, and so it is easy to establish that it faces west.*

above: *This front garden has two entrances, but the main one is toward the street, and so the garden faces east.*

which one the garden faces. Some gardens even have three or four regular entrances – perhaps a couple of backdoors and one or two gates. There's no need to take a strict survey to find out which entrance is used most. Just go outside and stand in your garden, and see which direction feels like the dominant one.

UNUSUAL GARDENS

As well as gardens with two or more entrances, there are other gardens that don't fit the pattern. You can feel intuitively that they face in a direction that is not necessarily the direction of the entrance. An example might be a garden built on a cliff top that clearly faces out to sea rather than back toward the house. Another would be a garden that faces down a hillside away from the house. Once again you should trust your own instincts – if you feel your garden faces in a certain direction, then you will probably be right.

Front and Back Gardens

SUPPOSE YOU *have more than one garden, or more than one section of garden? Perhaps you have a back garden that wraps around the side of the house and into the front garden. Is that one garden or two? Maybe the front and back gardens are completely separate. Or maybe you are lucky enough to have a lot of land and several distinct areas. Are you meant to treat all of these as one garden for feng shui purposes, or are you supposed to assess them all separately?*

THE FENG SHUI OF THE HOUSE AND GARDEN

The feng shui of your house influences your life from a personal point of view; your garden is the outer aspect of your house, and its feng shui influences the more public aspects of your life. So the area of your garden that influences your relationship affects the everyday, visible aspects of the relationship rather than your private attitude toward it, which is influenced by the house feng shui.

The best way to examine the feng shui of your garden is to treat your entire plot of land as a single unit. If you have a garden on more than one side of the house, this will probably mean including your house in the overall feng shui chart, where it will occupy one or more of the eight areas. This is by far the most balanced approach to adopt.

YIN AND YANG GARDENS

However, this is another example of a time you may need to use your intuition. If you really feel you have more than one garden, assess the feng shui separately and regard the front garden as yang and the back as yin. While both gardens influence the outer, visible aspects of your life, the front garden influences the most public, open side, while the back garden relates to the side that only your family and close friends see.

above: *If you feel that the back and front gardens are so separate that they cannot be treated as parts of one whole plot, then view the back garden as the more private side of your life.*

But regarding the front and back gardens as separate is a more fragmented way to look at your life, which may be reflected in a lifestyle in which different aspects – work, family, friends – are kept very separate. If you find that these aspects of your life aren't as integrated as you would like them to be, can you see a way of adapting the design of your gardens so that they feel more like a single unit divided up rather than two or more separate gardens?

The Pah Kwa
and the Garden

*N*OW IT'S TIME *to find out which aspects of your life are influenced by each area of your garden. You do this by taking a simple plan of your garden and overlaying the pah kwa octagon onto it. The pah kwa is divided into eight sections, each of which represents a different aspect of your life. By seeing where each of these eight sections falls, you can establish which part of your garden will influence each area of your life.*

FITTING THE PAH KWA WITH THE GARDEN PLAN

This is where you need to know which way the garden faces. Take the pah kwa octagon and lay it on top of the plan of your garden so that the "fame" section of the pah kwa faces the same way the garden faces. If your garden faces north-west, for example, the fame section of the pah kwa will be in the northwest. You can then read off each of the other seven sections and see which part of the garden each sits on top of. This is the part of the garden that influences that part of your life.

opposite: *The beneficial flow of ch'i needs light, provided here by a candle. Without this energy-stimulating token, the warrior could be a forbidding figure.*

For example, if the "fame" section is in the northwest, the north of your garden will influence your health and happiness, and the west will influence your wealth. You can continue around the pah kwa (illustrated on the next page) to find out which part of your garden relates to the other areas.

MISSING PIECES

Suppose your garden isn't a regular shape? If you have an L-shaped garden, you may have entire aspects of your life that don't marry up with parts of your garden at all. If this is the case, it is likely that these aspects of your life are missing or diminished. People who are very prone to illness often find that the health section of their garden is missing.

If an area is missing in your garden but not your house, it often means that the related aspect of your life is private or secret – it is present in your personal, house feng shui, but not in your more public, garden feng shui. For example, if you are having a love affair that you are keeping very quiet for some reason, you might find that your house has a relationship section but your garden is lacking one.

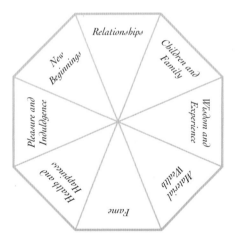

Figure 2: The pah kwa

Overlay the pah kwa on to a plan of your garden to see where each aspect falls.

ENLARGED SECTIONS

Many gardens come in odd shapes. They have extra bits tacked on, or they stick out on one side, or you have acquired a paddock beyond the original garden, or a bit of land at the front that used to be next door's driveway. These sections often protrude from the plan after you have overlaid the pah kwa on the main section of your garden.

If any of the pah kwa sections extends into a large part of the garden, this means that the aspect of your life in question is well blessed. People with plenty of money often have an enlarged wealth section, and those with large families tend to have extra space in the children area of their garden.

INCLUDING YOUR HOUSE IN THE PLAN

If your garden surrounds your house, or falls on more than one side of it, you may well have had to include the house in the overall plan. In this case, some of the eight life areas covered by the pah kwa will have fallen within the house rather than the garden. This means that your life is more complete and integrated than it would be if your garden were treated as a separate area.

However, certain parts of your life don't fall into the public sphere at all. If the wealth area of your life falls within the house, maybe you earn your money

above: *Choose the area carefully when positioning a bench on which you want to sit and relax.*

in a private way. Perhaps you work alone, maybe even from home, or perhaps your wealth comes from a source you keep private – an inheritance, maybe, or perhaps you play the stock markets.

USING THE EIGHT AREAS

You now have a plan that divides your garden into eight areas (or fewer if any are missing). Now you know which aspect of your life is influenced by each part of the garden, you can use your garden to make

the most of its feng shui. Put the children's swing in the area that governs children and family, put the barbecue in the pleasure and indulgence section, and so on. Even if your garden is small and you want to use the whole garden for one purpose, you can still incorporate these areas into the way you use it. Suppose you want to use the whole garden for meditation; place a seat in the part of the garden most important to your meditation – wisdom, perhaps, or health and happiness.

The Eight Enrichments:
The Eight Areas of the Pah Kwa

YOUR GARDEN *is divided into eight sections by the pah kwa that you have overlaid on a plan of your garden. The ch'i needs to flow smoothly in and out of all parts of the garden to create good, harmonious feng shui, and we will look at how to achieve this later. But in addition, you will achieve the maximum benefit from the feng shui of your garden if you use each area for activities related to the part of your life that it governs.*

It would be unwise, for example, to put your compost heap in your relationship area – you throw kitchen waste and dead plant material on it. What will that do to your relationship? It is likely to rot along with the compost. However, you could put the compost heap in your wisdom and experience area, where the value of all the material in it will gradually combine to create an accumulated wealth of goodness to bestow on the next generation of plants.

1 Fame: This area of the garden governs your reputation, so it is the ideal place to entertain people you want to impress, or to grow flowers for showing off. If you exhibit fruit or giant vegetables at shows, cultivate them here.

Don't use this area for anything private, such as a potting shed to hide in when you're feeling stressed, or a seat for quiet contemplation – you're very likely to be interrupted.

2 Health and happiness: This is a good place to relax and recharge your batteries, so put a chair or bench here and perhaps a pool with a fountain or water feature – the sound of running water will help to refresh you. This is also a good location for a herb garden, especially if you grow herbs for healing, or relaxing herbs such as lavender.

opposite: *Grow medicinal herbs in the area of health and happiness. The green color of a lawn reinforces the relaxing qualities of this area.*

above: *This relationship area has all that's needed to bring in a new partner, with seating for two at a round table, and a single fruit tree. The circle of neat brick paving and the clever lighting promote ch'i. However, the seats should be positioned with their backs toward the fence.*

3 Pleasure and Indulgence: This is the part of the garden for having fun. Use it for whatever you like to indulge in most. Maybe you should put your barbecue here and entertain your friends – your parties are likely to be a big success. In fact, you may have diffi-culty getting people to go home at the end of the evening. If you can afford it, this is the place for a swimming pool or an outdoor jacuzzi or hot tub.

4 New Beginnings: If you're the type that likes to tinker with making things in your toolshed, this is a good place to site it. Or you could use this area for a greenhouse or seed bed for raising young plants. This is also the best area for keeping your trash cans, since it symbolizes a continual throwing out of the old to be replaced with something new.

5 Relationships: Use this part of your garden for activities you and your partner like to share. Perhaps you like to tend the vegetables together, or maybe you prefer simply to sit and talk. Whatever your choice, make sure you can do it in this section of the garden. If you are single but would like to find someone to share a relationship with, keep this part of your garden well tended and free of weeds, and plant it with perennial plants, or with a tree that will bear fruit in its first season or two, such as an apple tree.

6 Children and Family: If you have children, this is the place to put their sandpit, swing, wading pool, and any other outdoor toys. Keep a grassy area clear for them to play on or, if this area is full of trees, build the children a tree house. Make sure the area is as safe as possible, and check that any boundary fences or walls are in good repair. If you have no children but do have a dog, this is the place to let it play freely.

7 Wisdom and Experience: This part of the garden is the place for learning and growing both mentally and spiritually. If you like to sit and read in the garden, do it here. Or you may like to turn this into a meditation area. Keep your compost heap here if you can, and use the area as a trial ground for growing new varieties of plants or vegetables, if the soil is suitable.

8 Wealth: This means not only financial wealth but other material wealth and property as well. This is a good area to store patio furniture over the winter, and to keep valuable items such as the lawn mower. If you make money from your garden, by selling produce or flowers, grow them here. And if you are lucky enough to work from home, this is the place to work outside on a warm day.

Remedies in the Garden

WHERE THE FLOW *of ch'i in your garden is not as smooth and free as it should be, you will need to remedy this. Later, when we look at individual aspects and features of the garden, we will discuss how you can tell when a remedy is needed. There are eight types of feng shui remedies, and you need to decide which is the most appropriate in each case. This decision depends on which section of the garden the problem area falls in, and the nature of the problem.*

1 Light: Ch'i flows badly in any area that is too dark, so this can be remedied by introducing more light with the use of

above: *Here the brightly colored rounded screen breaks the rectangular shape and promotes the flow of ch'i.*

opposite: *Using a statue, the sound of bells, and light from a candle are some of the ways of improviong feng shui.*

mirrors or garden lights, or by simply clearing or cutting back plants. Water is also a useful way to bring reflected light into the garden. Add a pool, a stream, or a fountain to stimulate the ch'i. Light remedies work particularly well in the south section of the garden.

2 Sound: Where the flow of ch'i is stagnating, it can be broken up using sound. You can use wind chimes, made of either bamboo or metal, or perhaps the sound of a stream or fountain. Or you could use the sound of birds or animals – a bird feeder will encourage birds to use the area. Sound remedies are at their most effective in the northwest.

THE FIVE ELEMENTS

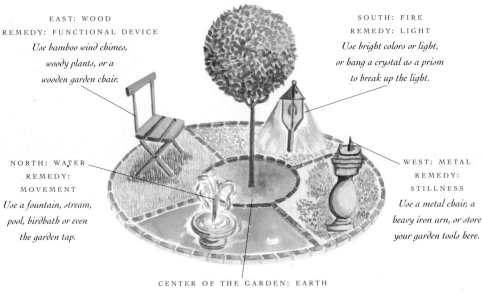

EAST: WOOD
REMEDY: FUNCTIONAL DEVICE
Use bamboo wind chimes,
woody plants, or a
wooden garden chair.

SOUTH: FIRE
REMEDY: LIGHT
Use bright colors or light,
or hang a crystal as a prism
to break up the light.

NORTH: WATER
REMEDY:
MOVEMENT
Use a fountain, stream,
pool, birdbath or even
the garden tap.

WEST: METAL
REMEDY:
STILLNESS
Use a metal chair, a
heavy iron urn, or store
your garden tools here.

CENTER OF THE GARDEN: EARTH
Use stone ornaments or pots,
or an old lichen-covered rock.

When there is more than one remedy for a particular problem, you need to choose the best one. For example, stagnating ch'i can be remedied using light, sound, color, movement, functional devices, or straight lines. So which is best? It depends on which area of your garden is affected. Try to use the device that is most at home in the area in question. Light remedies, for example, work especially well in the south.

The Chinese have five elements – fire, water, metal, wood, and earth – and each has its own direction. So also find a device to suit the element for that part of the garden. For example, water is the element of the north, and movement is the remedy that works best in the north. So think of a moving-water remedy here, for example, a fountain.

above: *This unusual earth sculpture makes a perfect stillness remedy in the center of the garden.*

3 Color: Color stimulates sluggish or stagnating ch'i to flow; red is a favorite color in China, and other bright colors such as orange and purple also stimulate ch'i. If the ch'i is being funneled down a straight path or is too overpowering, use greens, whites, cool blues, and soft pinks to calm it down. You can use suitably colored plants, or you might prefer to use colored or painted ornaments, pots, or lawn furniture. Color remedies work especially well in the northeast section of the garden.

4 Life: Sometimes ch'i has difficulty getting into corners. It can be encouraged to move in by something that is alive. Plants are clearly an ideal solution, but you could use a pond with fish in it, or a bird feeder or birdbath. Life remedies are best used in the southeast.

5 Movement: If ch'i is stagnating, or if it needs to be deflected, you can use movement to achieve this. Once again, you could encourage birds into the area, or add a fountain or stream, or a wind chime. Or grow plants or trees that move easily in the slightest breeze, such as

aspen trees. Use movement remedies in the north of the garden, where the sleepy ch'i often needs waking up.

6 Stillness: Where ch'i is overactive you can persuade it to slow down by placing something still in its path, in the form of a large heavy object. For this you could use a statue, a piece of sculpture, or a garden urn or pot. Stillness remedies work especially well in the west of the garden.

7 Functional Device: Any object that is active and performs a practical function helps to revive sleepy or stagnating ch'i. You might use a sundial, or perhaps the barbecue, or the garden tap. The part of the garden where functional devices work best is in the east.

8 Straight lines: Straight lines help to move ch'i along when it is inclined to linger. You can use straight paths to create horizontal straight lines. Vertical straight lines can be achieved using arches and obelisks, or by planting straight stemmed plants such as bamboo. Use straight line remedies in the southwest of the garden.

The Garden Entrance

THE ENTRANCE *to your garden is the main access for ch'i, as well as for visitors. What encourages visitors will also encourage ch'i. So you need to have a good look at the main entrance — and then any other entrances — and make sure that it is welcoming. You also need to consider the direction the entrance faces and the type of ch'i it receives, to make sure that the entrance suits the ch'i coming through it.*

THE SOUTH-FACING ENTRANCE

If your entrance faces south, it will attract lots of expansive yang ch'i. This is a good thing but it can become overpowering, so the entrance should be broad and open, but not too large or the ch'i will rush in too fast.

There are plenty of techniques you can adopt to slow down this overexuberant ch'i. Put an archway over your entrance or plant a tree beside it. Use a boundary which slows but doesn't block the ch'i, such as a trellis or an openwork fence. Avoid trees that block the flow of ch'i completely and choose ones with open branches that the ch'i can still flow through — fruit trees, perhaps, or maples. The dappled shade from these trees will also tone down the brightness of the yang ch'i.

THE NORTH-FACING ENTRANCE

The ch'i flowing from this direction is heavy and sleepy, and it needs all the help it can get to persuade it to come into the garden. Open up this entrance as much as possible, make the gateway fairly wide, and have a straight, or almost straight, path leading up to it.

Clear away any dark, overhanging trees or somber shrubs around the entrance, and create as open and expansive a feel as you can. If the entrance is hidden in the corner of the garden, could you move it out to a more open position? Simply moving a gate three or four feet out from the corner can make a huge difference. Movement remedies work

opposite: *The entrance to the garden is all-important and should be adapted according to the aspect.*

well in the north. Can you introduce some kind of movement near the gate such as a weathervane or feathery plants that move in the breeze?

THE WEST-FACING ENTRANCE

Ch'i from the west can be dangerous, and it is best to allow in only small quantities. So keep entrances on this side of the garden fairly small, and break up any ch'i that enters with wrought iron or lattice-work gates, or by forcing it to slow down as soon as it enters – a trellis screen or a tree just inside the entrance, with a path that has to bend around it, will check the flow of ch'i.

The most important thing is not to funnel ch'i from the west by creating straight paths, especially with pergolas or a run of arches leading from the gate. Don't try to block the ch'i out altogether with a solid door; every time it is opened the ch'i will rush in. In any case, a little ch'i from the west is a good thing. It is lively and promotes activity, which is beneficial in moderation.

THE EAST-FACING ENTRANCE

This ch'i is kind and protective and should be encouraged. You can keep entrances on this side of the garden open and expansive, but do keep a slight check on it or the garden can become so fertile it runs wild. Make sure there is at least a boundary on this side of the garden, even if it's only an open fence.

DOORS AND GATES

What sort of entrance gate should you have? In order for the ch'i to flow smoothly in and out, it is best to avoid solid doors. The main exception to this is where you have more than one entrance on one side of the garden and you want to block the flow of ch'i through one of them to prevent it from becoming too strong. Otherwise, use open-work gates of a suitable material. Wood is most at home in the east, and metal in the west.

The more open the gateway, the more easily the ch'i can flow through it. Waist-high gates allow ch'i to flow over the top, while full-height gates – especially set into walls, fences, or hedges – slow it down.

Remember that you can influence the flow of ch'i by the color you paint the gate. Bright colors stimulate the ch'i, and reds and oranges are good for encouraging yang ch'i from the south, especially if you can't create as open an entrance as you would like. Cooler blues and greens keep the ch'i flowing but are gentler, and more appropriate for slowing down dangerous ch'i from the west, or encouraging the gentle ch'i from the east.

above: *Wrought iron or latticework gates can be used to modify the flow of ch'i without blocking it. However, the gate should not be left open or it will be unable to fulfill this function.*

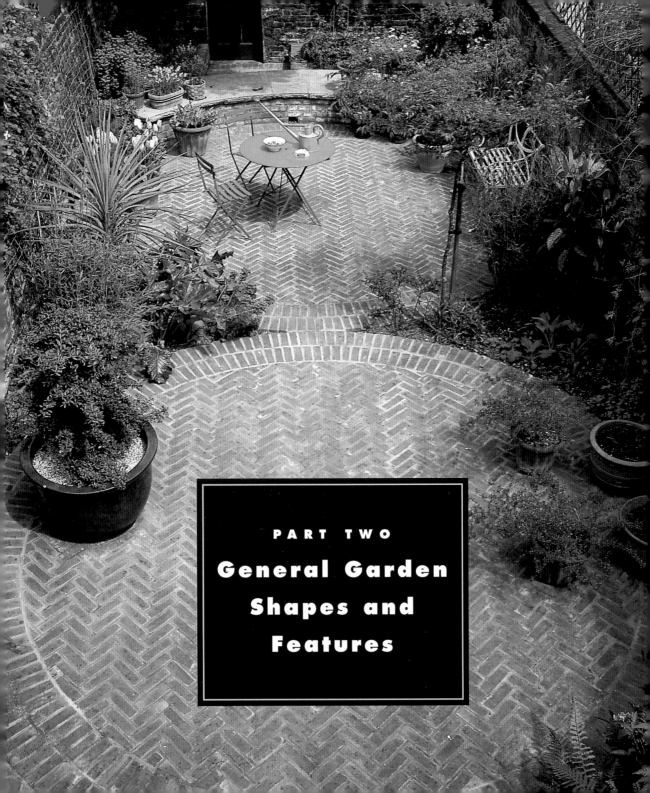

PART TWO

General Garden Shapes and Features

The Shape of the Garden

T HE OVERALL SHAPE *of your garden will have a strong impact on its feng shui. Is it a single, open shape that allows the ch'i to move smoothly, or is it full of angles and corners with an irregular shape that doesn't align comfortably with the pah kwa? Regular-shaped gardens are better for feng shui than gardens with irregular shapes – such as L-shapes or T-shapes – but there are remedies you can employ to give any garden good feng shui.*

REGULAR-SHAPED GARDENS

Ch'i likes to flow smoothly and be able to get into all the corners of your garden. So it's much better to have a garden with a straightforward, regular shape without sections jutting out, or angles that make it difficult for the ch'i to get around. Regular layouts also enable you to line up the pah kwa in such a way that there are no missing areas or enlarged sections. So the best shape for a garden is either circular or octagonal – but very few of us have gardens this shape. Square is the next most regular shape; a rectangular garden

opposite: *The regular rectangular shape of this garden is ideal, and the curved edges of the brick terraces also help to channel the ch'i.*

that is very long and thin will create enlarged pah kwa sections, so the closer to a square shape the better.

BENDS AND CURVES

Ch'i likes to flow in gentle curves, so avoid straight lines in your garden design. Take the front edge of your patio around in a curve rather than cutting straight across the garden. Garden buildings and structures are often square but you can soften straight edges of square and rectangular gardens with flowerbeds that curve where they meet the lawn. Have a circular or curved-edged lawn in the center of your garden. Use rounded rather than flat-topped arches to support climbing plants, and make ponds and pools round or curved rather than square. Allow streams to bend naturally rather than flow down straight channels.

The exception to this is where you need to funnel ch'i toward an area that is stagnating. For example, if you have a long, narrow section of garden that opens into a wider space, and the ch'i tends to stagnate, you could encourage the ch'i down the long section with a straight path or an avenue. When it reaches the end, curve the edges of the garden so that the ch'i can flow around and back out again.

IRREGULAR SHAPED GARDENS

It is quite possible to create good feng shui in a garden that is not a regular shape; it just takes a little more input on your part. You will need to encourage the ch'i to flow around the angles and into any deadends or corners. There are several techniques you can use to achieve this:

* If there is a sharp bend in the garden, make sure that any paths, lawn, or flowerbeds are curved rather than echoing the sharp angle of the garden shape

* Encourage the ch'i into corners and alleyways with a remedy that stimulates it. Try using light, sound, color, life, movement, or functional devices. Any of these will do but, if possible, use the one that is best suited to the direction of that part of the garden.

    LIGHT: *south*, SOUND: *northwest*,

    COLOR: *northeast*, LIFE: *southeast*,

    MOVEMENT: *north*, FUNCTIONAL DEVICE: *east*

* Design the area in a way that brings it together as one unified shape. Don't shut off any sections behind hedges, walls, or gates, but treat them as part of the overall design. Let the shape of the lawn curve in and out of any extra sections, or let the flowerbeds continue around corners. Don't change the material your paths are made from when you reach a corner, but use the same gravel, brickwork, or paving in the section that extends around the corner.

* Smooth off any sharp corners in some way. For example, suppose the garden goes around the corner of the house. You should grow a climber up the house to obscure the sharp corner where the two sides of the house connect. Or put a curved bench or flowerbed on the corner to encourage the ch'i to flow gently around.

above: *In a less formal garden, an irregularly curving lawn and bordering path encourage the flow of ch'i.*

SECRET CORNERS

Although you want your garden to have a fairly regular shape, if it is completely open the ch'i may be too active. Just like us, ch'i likes to be lured into secret parts of the garden, and tempted to see what is around the next curve. So don't be afraid to create parts of the garden that can't be seen all at once. Just make sure that they are easy to reach down curving paths or through archways, not stuck behind sheds or down alleyways.

Boundaries

THE BOUNDARY *of your garden is very important. All the ch'i that flows around your garden comes initially from the outside, and you have no control over it. It may arrive from an area of very poor feng shui. You can control the ch'i that reaches your house by improving the feng shui of your garden, but the only way you can control the ch'i that enters your garden is by creating a suitable boundary to encourage or deter it, speed it up or slow it down.*

BOUNDARIES AND THE PAH KWA

We have already looked at encouraging or discouraging ch'i from certain compass directions, but you also need to consider the pah kwa area that is affected. For example, if you find it difficult to make or to keep friends, you might find that the ch'i is not flowing well in the friends section of your garden. In this case, you could open up the boundary to encourage it.

Conversely, you might find that certain areas of your life are overactive. Suppose you never get any work done because you can't resist going out and enjoying yourself all the time.

Perhaps you could redress the balance a little by slowing down the ch'i as it enters your pleasure and indulgence area.

HIGH OR LOW, THICK OR THIN

There are two basic ways to vary the amount of ch'i that your boundary lets through. You can adapt the height of it; a tall fence, wall, or hedge blocks out more ch'i than a low one. If you want to encourage more ch'i from a particular direction, you can do it by lowering the boundary on that side of the garden. Perhaps your wealth area is inclined to stagnate, and you want to encourage the ch'i to flow around it more readily in order to pep up your finances. Reduce the height of the hedge or wall, or put up a lower fence.

above: *Using an open trellis for a boundary fence avoids blocking the flow of ch'i. The plants growing up the trellis soften the effect, and the leaves of a wisteria moving in the breeze help to enliven the area.*

The other way to influence the amount of ch'i flowing into the garden is by altering the density of the boundary. More ch'i flows through an open trellis than through a solid brick wall. A yew hedge keeps out more ch'i than a beech hedge. If you have an open fence or trellis and want to slow down the ch'i, plant close-growing climbers up it, such as ivy or Virginia creeper.

Light and Shade

LIGHT IS YANG *and shade is yin. The ch'i in your garden should contain a balance of yin and yang energies, so you need to make sure that the mixture of light and shade is well balanced. Ch'i flows from areas of yin to yang and back again constantly, like electricity in an alternating current, so it needs both these elements in order to keep moving smoothly. Make sure you both encourage sunlight and provide shade in your garden.*

CREATING A BALANCE

You can achieve a good balance by creating areas of both light and shade, but don't make the contrast too stark. Ch'i doesn't like to move from deep shade into

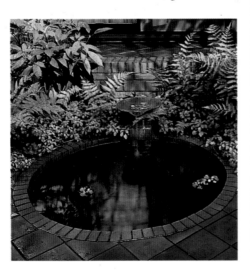

above: *Water can be used to introduce more light, and green ferns planted near the water give balance.*

blinding sunlight any more than you do. Try to grade the depth of light and shade in the garden so that you pass through light or dappled shade at the edge of the brightest areas.

Orchards tend to have excellent feng shui because the light is always dappled; you can reproduce this by planting fruit trees, or other trees that give dappled light such as willows or maples. A rose arch between a bright section and a shady section will give you broken light to smooth the transition between the two areas, or you could use a latticework screen to break up the sunlight.

TOO MUCH LIGHT OR SHADE

If there is too much bright yang light in the garden, create shade by planting trees or by adding an arch or pergola and

above: *Evergreens can make too much shade, but when neatly clipped in stepped and rounded shapes they produce a balanced blend of dark and light.*

planting roses, vines, or honeysuckle over it. If the light is only excessive in the summer, use a sunshade that you put up only when the sun is at its brightest.

While some shade in the garden is a good thing, it is never beneficial to have very deep, black shade such as the kind you get under conifers that put out branches close to the ground. The ch'i here cannot move at all.

You can prune – or even remove – trees and shrubs in shady areas. Or use light remedies, such as water, to bring reflected light into a shady area. Mirrors might look strange in a country garden, but they work well in a courtyard. Using a bright, sunny color such as white or pastels will also lift a shady area. Use colored pots, or paint walls, trellis, or benches to bring the color into the area.

Open Spaces

ALL GARDENS *should include some kind of open space, or the balance will be too yin. Ch'i needs open yang areas. Think how you would feel in a garden that had no open areas at all. The open space doesn't need to be in the center, but it shouldn't be tucked away in a corner. In many gardens an open space is created using grass. But the open area doesn't have to be a lawn; it could be a paved area, or even a pond.*

KEEPING IT IN PROPORTION

It is impossible to say what size the open area should be, since the important thing is that it should suit the garden. If you have three acres of land, a space just large enough for a table with a few chairs around it and no more is going to be inappropriately small. But if you have a small town garden, perhaps only 18 or 20 feet (6 or 7 m) square, the same amount of space might be ample.

The ch'i in your garden needs to balance open space with areas where paths curve between plants and buildings in the same way that it needs to balance light and shade. It doesn't want to funnel down from a wide open area to get through a tiny entrance. So keep any paths, arches, and gates broad where they lead away from open spaces.

WHAT KIND OF SPACE?

A circular, or roughly circular, open area in the middle of your garden is ideal. If the garden is large, you might have several open areas, connected by paths through garden or woodland areas. One of the best ways to treat a long, narrow garden is to divide it into two or three open areas with trees, buildings, or flowerbeds in between.

Some functional areas are naturally open; however, it is important not to fence these areas off. If you want to fence your swimming pool or your tennis court, or to net your vegetable garden, you should make sure that you have other open areas in the garden as well.

If you have room for a lawn this is ideal, since the color green is very calming, preventing the ch'i from

above: *Even in functional areas rounded shapes can be employed.*
An open surround can be used to define the space for a calming effect.

becoming overactive in all that open space. However, you could use other materials such as gravel, paving, or brickwork.

Another possibility is to create a pond in the center of your garden, leaving room for a path and a seat around it.

Paths

PATHS ARE ONE *of the most important features of almost any garden. Unless your garden is tiny, you are almost bound to have paths to get you from one part of it to another. Even if you have a large area of lawn, you usually find that you wear a path in it by regularly taking the same route across it from the backdoor to the garden gate, or from the greenhouse to the toolshed. Ch'i also travels down these paths, so you need to insure that they take the ch'i where it needs to go, at the speed it needs to travel.*

Straight paths encourage ch'i to flow down them, and to flow fast. This is a good thing if the area at the end of the path is prone to stagnate the ch'i, since a straight path will keep the ch'i flowing. If you have a shady area, or an area tucked away from the rest of the garden where the ch'i cannot easily get to it, a straight path will help to bring this area into the garden as a whole. If the ch'i is already flowing well, however, your paths should curve gently since ch'i likes to flow in smooth curves.

You need to take into account the direction from which the ch'i is flowing. If it comes from the south it will bring

above: Since straight lines enable ch'i to hurry along, meandering paths are best in most circumstances.

lively yang ch'i into the area. If the area is in the north of the garden it may be full of sleepy yin ch'i, and an injection of yang ch'i is just what it needs. In this case, a straight path will be beneficial.

However, if the area in question is your relationships area, for example, and you are one of those people who is prone to the temptation of affairs or who has too

opposite: A straight path leading to a shady area brings the area to life, but such paths have to be used with care, or they can channel too much unwanted energy.

many relationships to choose from, the last thing you need is to bring all that active, lively yang ch'i into your relationship area. You would be far better off finding ways to calm down the ch'i in this area, or encourage wise ch'i from the east rather than exuberant south ch'i. Make sure that any paths from the south bend and curve to slow down the ch'i.

It is never a good idea to speed up dangerous ch'i from the west by encouraging it down a straight path; avoid this kind of path running directly from the west side.

PATHS RUN BOTH WAYS

Don't forget that any path that carries ch'i from south to north also carries it back again. Some paths clearly run in one direction even though they can be used in both, while others are more balanced. A path running downhill from an open area of lawn, narrowing as it goes, is obviously leading away from the lawn even though you could clearly travel the other way along it.

But a straight path connecting two open areas is flowing both ways. If it carries ch'i along it in one direction, it will carry it the other way too. The closer to one side of your garden it is, the more

dominant the ch'i from that direction will be. In the east of the garden, for example, a straight path carries more easterly ch'i along it toward the center of the garden than westerly ch'i going the other way. Remember to take this into account if you construct a straight path.

SHAPES AND MATERIALS

Generally speaking, ch'i prefers wide paths. If there are branches or arches overhead, these should be high enough to allow you to get underneath without ducking. If the path leads away from an open area it should be broad so that the entrance to it makes a smooth transition from the open space. However, it may narrow a little farther on, as it curves around into more secret areas.

Paths can be made of many materials, but be aware of the contrast of light and shade that is needed in the garden. In a shady area, perhaps full of dark green foliage, a light-colored path — maybe gravel or grass — creates a contrast and brings light into the area. Darker paving materials are more suitable in areas that are too bright and need toning down.

A change in paving materials creates a break that slows down ch'i, sometimes excessively so. For example, a dark, relatively narrow path between heavy foliage, which leads off an area of grass, can deter ch'i and cause it to stagnate along the path. Better to make the path of grass as well, or to have the darker paving run around the edge of the lawn and then branch off to run down the pathway between the foliage.

above: *Curving paths are generally preferable to straight ones. A variety of materials or shapes will slow down the flow of ch'i.*

Beds and Borders

FLOWERBEDS ARE *an attractive feature in most gardens. They often occupy more space than anything else, except perhaps the lawn. Many gardens simply have strips of flowerbeds along the edges, but the shape of the flowerbeds is important, and deserves more thought than this. It is also possible to create island beds in the center of lawns or paved areas, which have a strong effect on the feng shui of the garden.*

THE SHAPE OF THE BEDS

Generally speaking, the edges of beds and borders should follow gentle curves rather than straight lines. The exception to this, as with paths, is in places where

above: *Regular shapes are best for flower beds. Where an area may need quieting, plenty of green plants should be used.*

opposite: *Ovals and circles are perfect for island beds in areas where no special balancing remedy is needed.*

you want to encourage the ch'i to flow faster to direct it toward an area of stagnating ch'i, or to bring a particular type of ch'i into that part of the garden. Straight edges to flowerbeds make a good straight-line remedy, which is most at home in the southwest.

Wide flowerbeds are better than narrow ones, although they should not be too wide or the ch'i will lose its direction and its flow. An ideal width is between 3 and 6 feet (1 and 3 m), depending on the proportions of the garden as a whole.

BORDERS

If you have a border – a flowerbed backed by a wall, trellis, fence, hedge, building, or other solid structure – the back edge of it will probably be a straight line. Unless you happen to need a

above: *The choice of materials, as well as plants, pots and sculptures, is important. Here darker pebbles are used to slow down the flow of ch'i in the straight path that cuts through the first circle and leads on the the circular seating area.*

straight-line remedy in this area, you will need to soften this. The best way to do this is to plant shrubs or bushy plants along the back, varying the distance they project forward, to create a second line along the back that is not as straight. Even if you have a beautiful old wall you want to show off, you can still soften the straightness of it by training fruit trees along it.

ISLAND BEDS

Island beds that can be approached from all sides are usually sited in a lawn or a paved area. These should be regular rather than abstract in shape. If you need a straight-line remedy in this area you can use a square or rectangular bed, but otherwise go for an oval or circular bed. If this part of your garden is already nicely in balance, use a circular island bed.

EDGING FLOWERBEDS

It is often practical to mark the dividing point between the flowerbed and the path, paving, or lawn next to it with some kind of edging. This can be a change in height, or it might be edging tiles, stones, or boarding.

A change of height encourages the ch'i to flow from the higher to the lower part. So flowerbeds that are raised above the path will allow ch'i to spill onto the path below. This can create a vertical funnel, which needs to be broken up. Grow plants that trail over the edge of the wall that holds the flowerbeds back, and keep the ch'i up in the flowerbeds with tall straight plants at the back of it and plenty of light, bright colors and pale foliage plants in front.

Any form of edging material inhibits the flow of ch'i from the path or lawn to the flowerbed and back again. If you want to use edging tiles or stones along your flowerbeds, make sure that the feng shui of both the beds and the paths are already in balance.

VEGETABLE BEDS

There is one area where straight beds can be hard to avoid, even if you don't want to use straight lines in that part of the garden. Vegetable beds are traditionally square or rectangular so that the vegetables in them can be planted easily in straight rows. But there are ways of avoiding introducing too many straight lines and thereby directing the ch'i too fast into the vegetable garden.

You can arrange the beds at right angles to each other so that the ch'i is channeled in different directions. Do this using plenty of smaller beds rather than a few large ones, and you create a layout that is almost like large-scale brickwork or paving. Another option is to create circular or semi-circular beds divided into segments, each of which can then be planted in straight rows. You can improve the feng shui further if you place an object or ornament at the center of the bed for the ch'i to flow round: a circular sundial, a large round pot, or a statue in a design with plenty of curves.

above: *Vegetable beds are a challenge, but softening their straight edges will enhance the feng shui.*

Functional Buildings and Objects

THERE ARE CERTAIN BUILDINGS *that you may need to have in your garden, such as toolsheds and greenhouses. You need to decide where to site these buildings so that they will create good feng shui, and you also need to decide what the building should look like. Should you make a feature of them or should you hide them? The same questions apply to functional objects such as trash cans, compost bins, and bonfire piles.*

SITING THE TOOLSHED

You need to consider the function of the building in question and then study the eight areas of the pah kwa to see which is the most suitable for the building. What do you keep in the toolshed? If you use it to store your gardening tools, put it somewhere that suits your approach to gardening. Do you see gardening as a pleasure and luxury? If so, you can keep your tools in your pleasure and indulgence areas. Or perhaps gardening is more of a meditation for you – in which case you might feel that your health and happiness area is a more appropriate place to keep the toolshed.

If you use your shed to tinker with bits of engines, or to keep electrical equipment for making and repairing things, you might prefer to keep it in your wisdom and experience area. Or if you make money from the things you construct in your toolshed – selling specialist car parts or antique garden tools – you should consider positioning the shed in your wealth area.

THE GREENHOUSE

Of course you need your greenhouse to face the right direction to catch the sun. But that isn't the only consideration in siting it. What do you use your greenhouse for? If you are bringing on your plants, put it in an area of new beginnings. But if you use your greenhouse

opposite: *The most mundane greenhouse can be brought into harmonious relation with the garden by the thoughtful use of plants.*

mostly to overwinter tender plants, you could put it in your wisdom and experience area, where you can work with the plants and learn to help them through the cold season. If you regard your plants as an extension of your family, as many gardeners do, talking to them and treating them as individuals, you could site your greenhouse in your children and family area. If you use it for herbs, put it in your health area.

TRASH CANS, COMPOST BINS, AND BONFIRE HEAPS

These items are all potentially damaging to feng shui in the wrong place. You don't want to find you are throwing away your reputation by putting your trash can in your fame area, burning money by siting your bonfire pile in your wealth area, or that your relationship is rotting away with your compost heap.

The best position for your trash can is in your area of new beginnings, since by constantly throwing things out you must be always introducing new items. However, you must make sure that the trash can is emptied regularly. If you miss the garbage collection for any reason, don't leave the rubbish for another week – take it to the dump yourself.

above: *The design of this compost bin allows the ch'i to flow through without stagnating.*

You can put your bonfire pile in your fame area, since by setting fire to it you are lighting a beacon that will attract people to you; you could say that you are putting your name in lights. Put your compost heap in your wisdom and experience area, since it will be used to impart all of its accumulated goodness to the next generation of plants.

DESIGNING YOUR BUILDINGS

It's no good thinking you can hide your toolshed around a corner, tucked away. The ch'i will be unable to reach it properly and will stagnate, along with all the activities the shed is supposed to serve. However, it is a good idea to soften the shape of the shed. Most are very angular, which ch'i doesn't like. An octagonal-shaped shed is ideal, but you can improve any shed by planting climbers up it, perhaps on a trellis. Use clematis or roses, or perhaps honeysuckle. The aim is not to smother the shed, merely to soften it. If the shed

below: *Clematis softens this garden toolshed, but the path leading up to it ensures that ch'i will still flow into it.*

is in a corner where there is a danger of ch'i stagnating, use a color remedy and paint it pale green or blue or, if it is in the south of the garden, a more vibrant yellow or red.

Greenhouses vary less in design than sheds; they are all primarily glass. However, remember that each element has its own direction. Use wooden-framed greenhouses in the east of your garden and metal-framed greenhouses in the west. A long, thin greenhouse will act as a straight line to direct ch'i, so be aware of this. If the feng shui of this part of your garden is already balanced, use a regular-shaped square or octagonal greenhouse.

Buildings for Pleasure: Decorative Buildings and Structures

MANY GARDEN STRUCTURES *are purely ornamental. When the weather is hot, there's nothing better than sitting in a cool summerhouse, or in the shade of a gazebo or pavilion. A greenhouse has to catch the sun, and a toolshed has to be close to where you want to use the tools. But it is far easier to position and design pleasure buildings to maximize the feng shui benefits, since you don't have any practical functions to accommodate.*

BUILDING SHAPES

You want the ch'i to flow around your buildings smoothly and harmoniously, so you need to construct them in shapes that are made up of curves rather than sharp angles. Ch'i loves circles, so why not have a round gazebo or summerhouse? Or you could opt for an octagonal building. If you decide to go for a square or rectangular shape, make sure the corners are rounded, or soften them by planting climbers up the corners of the building.

Remember you are working in three dimensions. It is not only the floorplan of the building that counts, but also its height and the shape of the roof. Make sure your building's height is in proportion to its width. Low, squat buildings can trap the ch'i inside them, while buildings that are disproportionately tall act as a straight line directing the ch'i upward.

ROOF SHAPES

Gazebos were invented in Persia and were always built with a hole in the center of the roof; they were intended for sitting in at night and viewing the stars. Open-roofed structures are very good for feng shui, since the ch'i can enter and leave freely through the sides, the door, and the roof.

opposite: *The perfect proportions, curving shapes and ivy cladding of this arbor, as well as the path that approaches it, make it a restful place for lingering in dappled shade.*

POSITIONING THE BUILDINGS

You can create a wonderful balance by placing a circular building in the center of a lawn or open area, which is roughly in the center of the garden. This creates the effect of a wheel hub that the ch'i can flow into, around, and out from any part of the garden. You need to make sure it doesn't have a whirlpool effect by constructing a building that calms down the ch'i – open-sided and open-roofed to break up the flow of ch'i, covered with scented plants that encourage the ch'i to linger a little before moving on, and painted a soft color.

But you might prefer to site the building in another part of the garden. In this case, match its function to the most appropriate part of the garden. Put a children's playhouse in the children pah kwa area; a summerhouse for reading, painting, or just thinking in a suitable area – wisdom and experience, or health and happiness; a pavilion for romantic alfresco dinners for two in the relationship area; a gazebo for entertaining friends in the pleasure and indulgence area, and so on.

below: *Open-sided buildings calm the ch'i and encourage it to linger in whatever area you choose to site the building.*

In China, roofs are traditionally built with the eaves curved upward in a distinctive style. The reason for this is to prevent the ch'i from pouring off the corners of the roof. The curving eaves slow the ch'i down as it reaches the edge, and allow it to flow gently beyond the edge of the building. This shape of roof can look very effective on summerhouses, gazebos, and pavilions, and helps to keep the ch'i flowing harmoniously.

OPEN-SIDED STRUCTURES

Some open-sided buildings are scarcely more than scaffolding for growing plants up, while others are more solid with walls made up of panels of trellis or lattice-work. These structures are beneficial to ch'i, since it can move in and out and around the building easily.

SCENT

If you decide to cover an open-sided building with climbing plants – which can create the dappled shade that ch'i likes – choose scented plants, since ch'i is attracted by sweet smells. Use honeysuckle, roses, or jasmine to encourage the ch'i to flow in and out of the building.

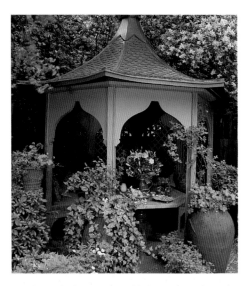

above: *In this very oriental looking summer house, situated in a dull northern area, the brightness of the flowers, and the food, bring more lively ch'i to the spot.*

COLOR

Remember that you can also stimulate or calm down the prevailing ch'i with the color you choose to use on a building. If you are in the sleepy, north section of the garden, you could use a bright color to encourage the lively yang ch'i from the south. Try a strong terracotta or vibrant, peacock blue if you don't like reds and oranges. If you have a building in the center of an open area such as a lawn, you can calm down the ch'i by painting it in cool pastel pinks, plums, or blues, or in a verdigris or soft green.

Water

ACCORDING TO THE CHINESE, *no garden can have good feng shui unless it contains water. Ch'i loves water, which attracts it and helps it to flow harmoniously. Water also brings wildlife into the garden, from birds to beetles, and any life is beneficial to feng shui. Moving water is best, but in a small garden a simple pond or even a birdbath will suffice. In a larger garden, fountains and streams bring good feng shui to their surroundings.*

USING NATURAL MATERIALS

Keep your water features looking as natural as possible: ch'i doesn't like plastic, fiberglass, and concrete. If you

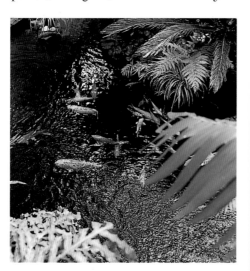

above: *Bright goldfish and gently swaying foliage bring life and movement to the still water of a garden pond.*

have to use these materials keep them hidden, and make sure that any visible structures are made of stone, wood, or earth. The shape of the water features should be as natural as possible. Unless you are creating a straight-line remedy, ponds and pools should have a curving shape, and streams should meander.

You can create places to sit beside your water features, or as part of them. Build an earth bank along the side of a stream, or a raised stone edge around your fish pond to sit on.

SAFE WATER FEATURES

If you have small children, you will want to be very careful about having water features in the garden. But there are ways of combining water and children

THE EIGHT REMEDIES

You can introduce water to your garden in all sorts of ways – streams and pools, lakes and fountains, swimming pools, birdbaths, and goldfish ponds. Water is the one feature you can use in your garden to provide any of the eight feng shui remedies you need.

LIGHT The reflection of sunlight moving on the surface of water brings light into dark areas of the garden and helps to lift them. Use a water feature in which the water moves constantly to make the most of the reflected light, such as a gently bubbling fountain.

SOUND You can create any sound from splashing to trickling, cascading to bubbling, using water features. If the ch'i is stagnating in any part of your garden, add a water feature that makes a noise to help keep it moving.

COLOR You can pep up sluggish ch'i with a shallow pool lined with brightly colored tiles, or with a ceramic birdbath glazed in a suitable color. If you don't like using vibrant colors in the garden you can always opt for traditional bright white.

LIFE Almost any water feature encourages wildlife. A stream or natural pond encourages a wealth of insects, from dragonflies to water beetles. Frogs and toads are also likely to be attracted. You might even be able to keep ducks on your pond. But even a feature as small as a birdbath attracts life. Or you could have a goldfish pond; the Chinese associate fish with money, so a goldfish pond in your wealth area is especially beneficial.

MOVEMENT Where you have life, you have movement. So any water feature that attracts wildlife will produce movement that stimulates ch'i. Or you could install a fountain, or a feature with moving water such as two pools connected by a stream. The water element is at home in the north, and this is also the place where movement remedies are at their most effective. So these remedies are ideal in the north of your garden.

STILLNESS Water doesn't have to be on the move. A stone trough or a shallow pool filled with water can be a cooling, still remedy to calm down ch'i that is moving too fast. If you are using water to create stillness, put it in a heavy, solid stone trough or a stone-lined pool with a simple rounded shape.

FUNCTIONAL DEVICE If you need a functional device to revive sleepy ch'i, how about a fountain? If you don't have room for a fountain, something as simple as a garden tap or hose will do the trick.

STRAIGHT LINE You can create a straight-line remedy by constructing a straight-sided channel for water to flow down from its source into a pool. Or, if you want a vertical straight line, you can install a fountain that shoots a jet of water into the air.

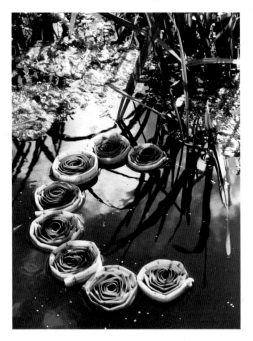

above: *Smooth, floating coils of green and white encourage the gentle flow of ch'i on still water.*

above: *A boat-shaped basket steadies the flow of moving water, while the bright blue binding enlivens the shade.*

safely. You could install a water feature with a little water bubbling up through an arrangement of stones or cobbles and then seeping back down, so that there is no standing water, or a fountain that spills water onto paving where it runs away through cracks in the ground. Or you could have a water channel only half an inch deep.

opposite: *The sound of a splashing fountain, as well as the sparkle of the moving water, enliven a shaded area that could otherwise be too still.*

These kinds of features are easy to create using inexpensive pumps that you can buy from garden centers. You could have a birdbath mounted securely out of reach of small children, or a winding channel of water that is fed with such a gentle supply that it isn't deep enough to be a safety hazard; you can keep the level of water down to as little as a quarter or half inch. This is still enough to create a cool flow of water that will help the ch'i to move harmoniously.

Statues and Ornaments

Y OU CAN MAKE *a difference to the feng shui of your garden using individual features such as sculptures, urns, and mirrors. The shape and color of these will determine their effect on the ch'i, as will the subject matter of any statues or ornaments. Large, heavy items make excellent stillness remedies in parts of the garden where the ch'i is moving too fast. You also need to take into consideration the material the ornament is made of, since this will influence the part of the garden in which it will be most effective.*

Remember that different elements are most at home in different directions. If you have ornaments made of wood, these will be best in the east of the garden, the direction of the wood element. Metal ornaments are most at home in the west, while the earth element – statues or pots made of stone or terra cotta, for example – belongs in the center of the garden.

You can use statues and ornaments to bring stillness to a part of the garden that has too much active ch'i; they are especially useful in the west where they help to calm down the potentially disruptive influence of the White Tiger. They can also be used as other remedies: any painted pots, ornaments, or sculptures can be used to bring a color remedy to the area. Glass and mirrors bring light to an area, and some objects can function as a straight-line remedy.

STATUES AND SCULPTURE

These could be made of wood, stone, or even metal. Large, heavy sculptures or statues make ideal stillness remedies, especially if they are a simple shape with a curving outline. A large stone ball would be a perfect stillness remedy.

opposite: A stone urn makes a good centerpiece. This one, made from local materials and using the local methods of wall building, is unusual and at home.

70

Think about the subject matter of any sculpture and put it in an appropriate place. Statues of children should go in the children section of the garden; a statue of lovers would be suitable in the relationship area. A bust of Dionysus, the Greek god of revelry, would be well placed in the pleasure and indulgence section; while the goddess of wisdom, Athena, would bring good feng shui to your wisdom and experience area.

NATURAL SCULPTURES

You don't have to buy sculptures and statues for your garden; you may well be able to find them. Look out for beautiful rocks or stones to decorate the top of a wall or to construct a homemade bird-bath. Or – if you can cope with moving it – find a large rock as a stillness remedy.

Pieces of driftwood have a natural beauty and tend to be worn by the ocean into natural feng shui shapes – curves and twists and bends. A large piece of driftwood would make an excellent still-ness remedy, or use several pieces to decorate the roof of a rustic summer-house; it will help to break up the ch'i so that it flows more gently off the roof. Or create wind chimes using pebbles and stones strung together.

POTS, URNS, AND TROUGHS

These can be made of wood, stone, metal such as lead, or terra cotta (avoid manu-factured materials such as plastic and fiberglass), or you can put pots inside a wicker or metal basket or stand. They can also be glazed or painted, so you can bring color remedies to areas that need bright colors to stimulate the ch'i, or cool colors to calm it down.

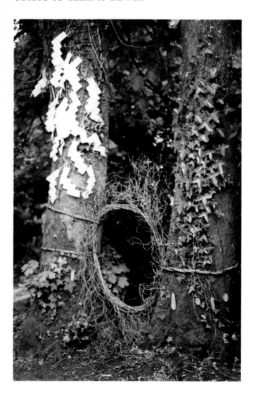

above: *The straight lines of these trees are softened by a willow sculpture and paper hangings to calm the ch'i.*

above: *Pebbles, smoothed by the sea, make a wonderful adjunct to naturally growing ivy leaves on a tree trunk.*

above: *Radiating leaves, centered on a heap of ripe berries bring color and roundness of form to the earth.*

Use round pots except where you want a straight-line remedy; square planters provoke the ch'i a little, so use them only where it is inclined to stagnate. Stone troughs worn down by age and rounded at the corners are excellent for feng shui especially if they are covered in moss. Collections of pots encourage the ch'i to flow around them as long as they are not cramped too close together. You can help to stimulate ch'i by arranging several pots in a row to create a straight-line remedy; this works best if the pots and their contents match each other.

MIRRORS AND GLASS

A mirror attached to a wall or fence helps to light up a shady area and introduces a feeling of space. This can be especially useful in a small courtyard or town garden. Disguise the hard edges of the mirror with climbing plants. Pay attention to what the mirror is reflecting; you want to see greenery, open spaces, water, trees, or beautiful flowers in it. You don't want to reflect the apartment block behind the house or the parking lot beyond the fence.

Glass ornaments can also bring light into the garden in other ways. For example, silver glass balls such as those hung on Christmas trees can light up a dark part of the garden. Or you can hang them under dark, evergreen trees which trap stagnant ch'i beneath them. Or you could float a glass ball, bubblelike, on the surface of a still pool of water to boost the amount of reflected light and bring some movement to the area.

Seats and Arbors

SOME PEOPLE LIKE *nothing better than to sit in the garden and relax. Others like being active in the garden – weeding and pruning, planting and mowing. But even the most active of us need simply to sit and enjoy the garden some of the time. Seating is an essential part of any garden, whether you have a single chair or half a dozen benches in different places. But deciding where to put your outdoor furniture takes thought to make sure you don't upset the balance with a badly positioned or poorly chosen chair.*

TAKING A REST

The first thing to bear in mind is that when you sit down you are resting. So decide which pah kwa areas you want to rest in. If you rest in your area of new beginnings, for example, you are likely to

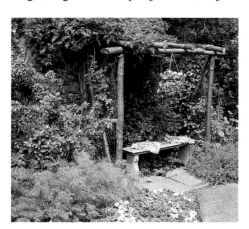

above: *A feathery-leaved jasmine softens the rustic poles that define this seating area to make a softly scented arbor.*

find that you start fewer projects. If you are already fraught and stressed and overworked this may be a good thing, but if you want to get new ideas and activities off the ground, this isn't the place for your lawn chair.

A seat in your children and family area is a good thing if you are prone to interfere in your children's lives too much and to be overprotective. But it would be unwise to sit and relax in this area if your children are already running wild and you can't keep track of where they are and what they're doing. If you want to have a seat in this area but don't want to change the balance of it, put in a swing. That way you can relax, but you have to put in just a little effort – you can't switch off altogether.

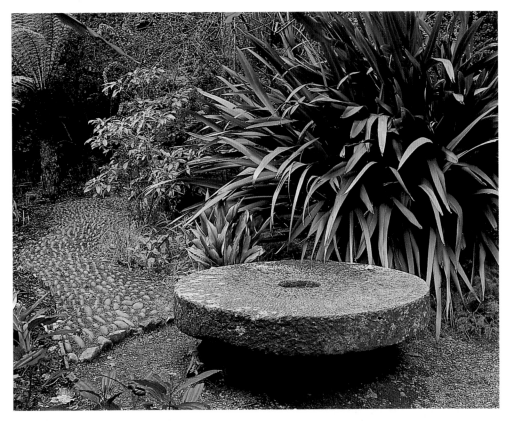

above: *A millstone used as a seat lends weight and stillness to an area in which ch'i flows smoothly and calmly.*

CHOOSING THE RIGHT SEAT

The shape of the seat, and any pattern on the bench, chair, or arbor, will affect the flow of ch'i. A long straight bench with horizontal slats acts as a straight line to speed up the ch'i, while a round chair with a curved back helps the ch'i to flow smoothly. A solid, heavy stone seat would make a good stillness remedy. Arbors make for very good feng shui as long as they are not too overgrown for the ch'i to flow in and out. Choose a shape with a rounded top, and use scented plants to attract ch'i. A scented arbor in the right place is excellent for the feng shui of your garden.

Trees

*I*F YOUR GARDEN *is anything but tiny, the chances are it has at least one or two trees in it. Anything living creates good feng shui, so trees are beneficial. They attract life and movement in the form of birds and insects and often numerous other creatures, as well as creating both movement and sound when they sway in the breeze. Having said all that, some trees are better for feng shui than others, so if you are planting new trees, consider carefully which variety to grow.*

STRAIGHT OR CURVY?

Ch'i likes to move in curves and bends rather than in straight lines, so the best kind of trees to grow are those whose overall shape is rounded rather than straight and tall. Oak trees are a classic feng shui shape, as are maples and magnolias. Tall, straight conifers are not as good for feng shui, and it's better to avoid them if you can. They are also often prone to create areas of dense, dark shade around their base in which the ch'i stagnates.

As well as the shape of the tree itself, you also need to consider the shape of the leaves. Once again, the more rounded they are, the better. Oak trees

have wonderfully curvy leaves, as do hawthorns and horse chestnuts. Pine trees have sharp needles, which can provoke ch'i; and trees such as willows that have long thin leaves are not as beneficial unless you need to stimulate the ch'i in that part of the garden.

TREES HAVE THEIR OWN CH'I

Everything has its own inherent ch'i, and the bigger and older a tree is, the stronger its natural ch'i. The wisdom of age is in such trees, and the Chinese say that an old tree should always be respected, no matter what its variety, or what its position in your garden.

Never chop down an old tree, or prune it heavily unless it is necessary to prolong the tree's life. The ch'i around

above: *The fallen petals form a circle round this magnolia, echoing its rounded shape and seeming to be a reflection of the almost translucent flowers.*

your garden has long since grown used to moving around the tree. There is no need to do anything unless the tree is a conifer whose lower branches sweep down to the ground, trapping stagnant ch'i beneath them. In this case, introduce a light remedy by hanging silver glass balls from the lower branches.

Shrubs and Climbers

SHRUBS AND CLIMBERS *are important because they bridge the gap between the tall trees and the lower flowers and border plants, making sure that the flow of ch'i can be even throughout the garden, vertically as well as horizontally. Shrubs and climbers help to give balance to the garden in terms of shape, and in creating patches of shade that are not as dominant as the large areas of shade often created by bigger trees.*

above: *Climbing plants are used to soften the wall and form a green background for a stone ornament.*

Shrubs are often the largest plants in small gardens, and in large gardens they are an important feature too. As with trees, you need to look first at the overall shape of the shrub, and choose ones with rounded shapes such as mexican orange blossom, philadelphus, or sage. After this, consider the shape of the leaves and choose shrubs with rounded rather than pointed leaves. Many shrubs and climbers are beautifully scented, and scent is an essential feature in a garden since it attracts ch'i and helps it to flow harmoniously.

EVERGREEN PLANTS

Color and life in the garden are important throughout the year, and evergreen plants are especially valuable for the feng shui of the garden. Shrubs that remain green all winter are well worth planting even if the plant or leaf shape isn't ideal, since the evergreen value outweighs this. Bay is an ideal evergreen, as are laurel, box, and privet. If evergreens are also scented, this adds even more to their value. This makes evergreen herbs such as rosemary and lavender ideal for keeping the ch'i flowing throughout the year, despite their spiky leaves.

TOPIARY

Many shrubs, such as box, can be cut and pruned into shapes that help the ch'i to flow. Use curvy shapes, such as spirals and balls. You can ease the flow of ch'i around the end of a hedge or a corner using topiary cut to a shape that helps the ch'i to move smoothly.

CLIMBERS

Climbers are ideal for softening edges and corners of buildings or garden structures, or you can grow them up trees to make them a little denser and slow down the ch'i. They also help to create dappled shade beneath arbors, arches, and gazebos. Thorny plants are best avoided except when, like roses, they have a strong scent that helps to soften the sharp effect of the thorns. Among the best climbers to grow

above: *Clematis, with its rounded flowers and leaves and winding tendrils, is an excellent shape to climb up a smooth tree trunk.*

are clematis and honeysuckle, both of which have beautifully curvy leaves, and scented wisteria and jasmine for their smell.

Evergreen climbers, such as ivy and some clematis and honeysuckle, create excellent feng shui throughout the year.

Border Plants

AMONG THE MAINSTAYS *of most gardens are the flowers, both annual and perennial, which grow in the flowerbeds. These bring life, scent, and color to the garden and attract wildlife such as insects and bees. As with trees and shrubs, you need to pay attention to the overall shape of the plant and to the shape of its leaves. Since the flowers of these plants are usually their prime feature, flower shape is also very important.*

FLOWER SHAPES

The rounder the shape of the flower the more it encourages ch'i to flow smoothly around it; anemones, poppies, daisy-shaped flowers, peonies, and roses are all good examples of this. Plants that put out flower spikes are better for stirring up stagnating ch'i; these include foxgloves (which are very useful in shady areas where the ch'i is sluggish), penstemons, and lupins.

Tall flowers with spiky leaves such as irises are best kept for situations where the ch'i needs stirring up, perhaps in the sleepy, north section of the garden. If you want to include tall flowers but don't want to provoke the ch'i, pick varieties with tall flower spikes but individual flowers that are round and help the ch'i to flow harmoniously. Examples of this kind of flower include hollyhocks and delphiniums.

Any sweetly scented flower is good for the flow of ch'i, regardless of the shape of the plant or the individual flower – the scent is more important. For this reason it is always a good idea to grow flowers such as lilies, pinks, sweet peas, and night-scented stocks.

THE GARDEN IN WINTER

It is very important to have some visible life in the garden throughout the year. Don't leave large areas of flowerbeds empty for several months at a time since this will have a deadening effect on the ch'i of the area, and the part of your life governed by that part of the garden will

above: *A well-planned border will have something to offer throughout the year.*
Taller irises and well-placed spiky leaves can wake up a border in a sleepy area of the garden.

stagnate through the winter. For this reason it is better not to devote large areas of garden to summer bedding plants, but to use such plants to fill gaps between other flowers. Plants that keep their foliage through the winter, such as euphorbias, are good winter mainstays.

Try to make sure that there are always a few flowers out in your garden at all times of the year. Grow winter flowering plants such as hellebores, bergenias (elephant's ears), winter-flowering heather, snowdrops, and primroses, and plenty of early spring bulbs.

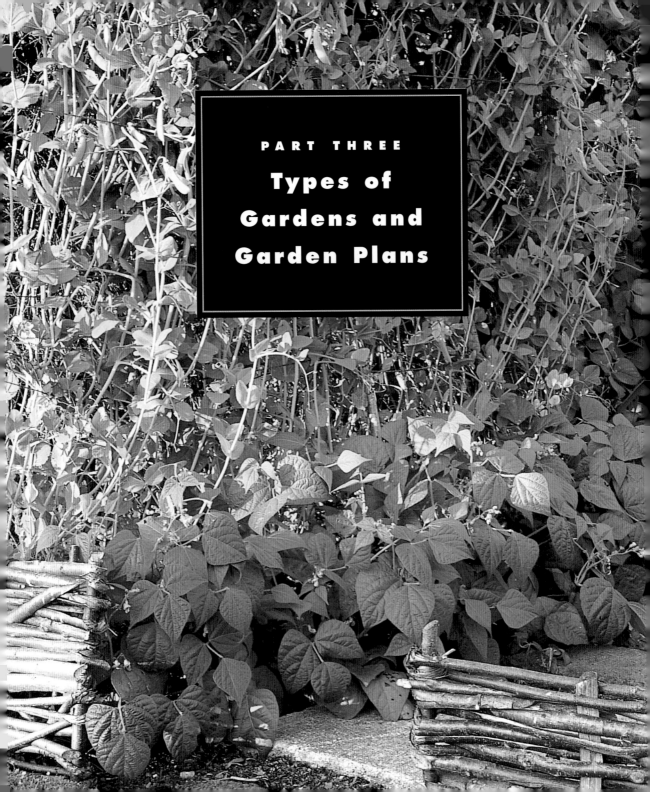

PART THREE
Types of Gardens and Garden Plans

The Productive Garden

Many PEOPLE LIKE *to grow their own vegetables and fruit – it's cheap, healthy, and fun. You can turn your whole garden over to productive growing, which works especially well if you grow flowers to cut for the house alongside vegetables and fruit. These pages suggest a design for a south-facing garden given over to productive growing. You can easily adapt the design if your garden faces in a different direction.*

This garden is square, but the overall design is based on a large circular bed in the center of the garden that has been subdivided into four sections. Three of these can be used for vegetables on a rotation basis, while the fourth can be used for permanent fruits such as raspberry canes and strawberry beds. At the center of this is a circular arrangement of metal arches, in gazebo style, which plants can be trained up. This gives the center of the garden a focal point for the ch'i to flow around and through.

The walls and fences around the edge of the garden have been softened by

opposite: Low wattle hurdles can be used to define the vegetable-growing area, their height, and their open texture, will lessen the flow of ch'i without blocking it altogether.

growing fruit trees up them. Shade is provided in the form of four arches, one at the end of each path leading to the central gazebo, each of which has climbing plants over it. The central gazebo itself also helps to provide shade.

The paths are made of brick laid in a herringbone pattern. The color is relatively dark to prevent the south yang ch'i from becoming too overpowering. The vegetable and fruit rows themselves are laid at right angles to each other in short rows, in order to prevent the lines from directing the ch'i too strongly in one direction. The overall circular theme of the garden design also counteracts any tendency for the ch'i to be funneled into straight lines.

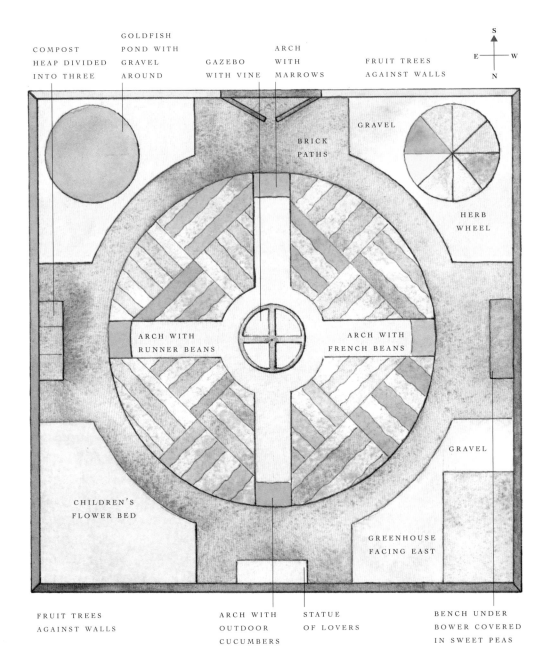

COMPOST
HEAP DIVIDED
INTO THREE

GOLDFISH
POND WITH
GRAVEL
AROUND

GAZEBO
WITH VINE

ARCH
WITH
MARROWS

FRUIT TREES
AGAINST WALLS

S
E   W
N

GRAVEL

BRICK
PATHS

HERB
WHEEL

ARCH WITH
RUNNER BEANS

ARCH WITH
FRENCH BEANS

GRAVEL

CHILDREN'S
FLOWER BED

GREENHOUSE
FACING EAST

FRUIT TREES
AGAINST WALLS

ARCH WITH
OUTDOOR
CUCUMBERS

STATUE
OF LOVERS

BENCH UNDER
BOWER COVERED
IN SWEET PEAS

THE EIGHT PAH KWA AREAS

1 Fame: Because the garden faces south, the entrance is in the fame area, which is the ideal place for it. Wrought-iron gates allow plenty of yang ch'i into the garden, but they break it up enough to stop it from becoming overpowering.

2 Health and happiness: This is an ideal position for the herb garden, the herbs arranged in a wheel set into gravel. Many herbs have healing properties as well as culinary ones, and this is the perfect place to grow them.

3 Pleasure and indulgence: A productive garden can be hard work to maintain, so here is a seat to sit back and enjoy the fruits of your labors – literally as well as metaphorically. This seat is covered by a bower with sweet peas growing over it. The smell attracts ch'i and the flowers can be cut for the house, since this encourages the plants to keep flowering.

4 New beginnings: This is the position for the greenhouse, set into gravel, which is lighter than the brick paths to attract the ch'i into the corners of the garden. The greenhouse faces east to catch the morning sun before it gets too hot.

5 Relationships: The relationship area contains a statue of two lovers embracing. It also forms a focal point since it can be seen through the archways as you enter the garden.

6 Children and family: This is the place for the children to have their own flowerbed where they can grow sunflowers, french beans, and other flowers and vegetables that are fun for children. You could also add a small tool store for them to keep their own equipment in.

7 Wisdom and experience: This part of the garden contains the compost heap. A productive garden produces plenty of waste material, which can be used to help the garden to continue producing healthy and tasty crops. This is a good place for the compost since it will develop and improve over time.

8 Wealth: A productive garden needs a pond to attract wildlife. If you're lucky, you may even attract frogs and toads, which will eat slugs and other pests. The Chinese associate fish with money, since the words for 'fish' and 'money' are very similar, so a fish pond in your wealth area is considered to be very lucky.

A Garden for Entertaining

IF YOU HAVE *lots of family or friends whom you like to entertain, you may well want a garden geared primarily toward this. There's no reason at all why a garden of this nature shouldn't have perfect feng shui, as long as you make sure that you use each part of the garden in the most appropriate way. The west-facing garden here has been designed to accommodate different kinds of activities for relaxing with friends.*

The most important first step with this garden is to calm down the potentially disruptive ch'i from the west where it enters the garden. This has been done by using a full-height wooden gate that is solid at the bottom and has lattice-work at the top. This slows down the flow of ch'i before it comes into the garden.

One of the best ways to deflect ch'i from the west is to slow down its approach to the garden by placing a screen a little way inside the gate. This not only forces the ch'i to bend and curve in order to reach the garden, but it also helps to provide privacy if the gate opens onto a road or other public area. Here, the job is done with climbing plants. The ch'i is directed toward the still, calm goldfish pond which helps to calm it further.

Once inside the main part of the garden there is a large central lawn area for playing games, for children to camp out, or simply for sunbathing; a patio area for eating and sitting out; and flowerbeds to insure that the entertaining takes place in beautiful surroundings. The garden is laid out using plenty of sweeping curves to attract the ch'i and keep it harmonious. A shady area has been created in one part of the patio with a pergola covered in climbers, and fruit trees at the bottom of the garden also provide dappled shade.

PERGOLA COVERED IN
JASMINE AND HONEYSUCKLE   PATIO

STONE
TABLE   LAWN

FRUIT
TREES

N   E   S   W

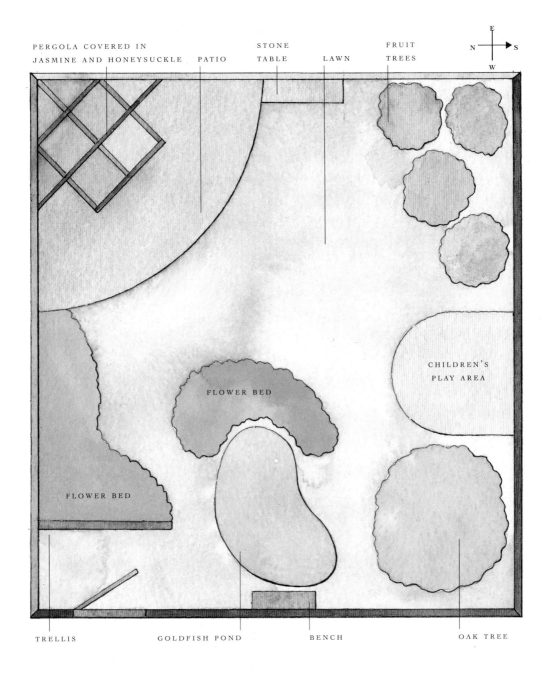

CHILDREN'S
PLAY AREA

FLOWER BED

FLOWER BED

TRELLIS   GOLDFISH POND   BENCH   OAK TREE

THE EIGHT PAH KWA AREAS

1 Fame: The entrance to the garden is in the west, which can make your reputation a little unpredictable. The trellis inside the gate helps to break up the dangerous ch'i from this direction which will help insure a more stable and reliable reputation.

2 Health and happiness: There is a flowerbed here, which should be filled with all your favorite plants, and plenty of scented flowers such as lilies, pinks, and lavender. You can also grow herbs in this bed.

3 Pleasure and indulgence: This is the main entertaining area. The barbecue can be placed somewhere on the patio, along with a table and chairs. The corner of the patio is shaded by a pergola extending from the walls and covered with scented jasmine and honeysuckle. The patio is made of flagstones that have space for flowers to grow up between them; this helps to break up what might otherwise be a stark expanse of stone. Use self-seeding flowers such as love-in-the-mist and nasturtiums.

opposite: An eating area in the round, where hard paving is softened by bushy, low-growing shrubs and flowering plants, makes for happy and successful entertaining of family and friends.

4 New beginnings: This area contains a fixed stone table against the wall for outdoor meals. Plates and salads can be set out here, and food can be prepared for the barbecue.

5 Relationship: This section contains a small orchard, insuring that your relationships will bear fruit. The orchard provides pleasant, light shade.

6 Children: This is a children's play area for entertaining children or the children of friends who are visiting. An area has been covered with wood chips to create a safe landing, and there is a swing, slide, and climbing frame.

7 Wisdom and experience: A large old oak tree stands in this corner of the garden. It provides cool shade, attracts wildlife and, like all mature trees, offers a wealth of wisdom and experience that can only influence the ch'i for your benefit and your family's.

8 Wealth: This part of the garden contains a fish pond, the classic Chinese symbol of wealth. It also has a bench to sit and watch the fish and enjoy the company in a quieter, more private fashion than on the patio. At the far end of the pond is a flowerbed that helps to obscure the view and create an added feeling of privacy.

A Romantic Garden

A ROMANTIC GARDEN *is one that attracts lovers with its charm, sweet scents, and peaceful atmosphere. These qualities also attract ch'i; therefore, a romantic garden that has been given a little thought about the positioning of various features is likely to have excellent feng shui. The romantic garden on these pages faces east, toward the kind, wise ch'i of the Green Dragon. It is not entirely regular in shape; the wealth section is missing and there is an additional section in the health and happiness area.*

This garden is full of sweeping curves to encourage the ch'i from one area to the next. There is a central, open area of green lawn, surrounded by a series of private areas such as an arbor, a pool, and an area for entertaining friends.

The plants in the flowerbeds contain plenty of scented flowers and also include shrubs to create sufficient height so that you can't see over the beds, creating privacy. The paths are of brick, laid in a herringbone pattern so that the ch'i is not encouraged in one straight direction only.

Like all good feng shui gardens, this one contains water. A fountainhead spills water from the wall into a curving stream that bends around under a bridge and into a pond, which is in the enlarged section of the garden. The movement of the water and the shape of the stream make this section feel like part of the whole garden, rather than a piece tacked on at the end. This impression is strengthened by the use of brick paving that links the area to the courtyard across the stream, inside the entrance gate.

THE EIGHT PAH KWA AREAS

1 Fame: The gateway is a broad, double gate at waist height only, to let in plenty of gentle, wise ch'i from the east.

2 Health and happiness: This is the enlarged area, which has been incorporated into the garden. It contains a pond with a raised edge for sitting on, where the sound and freshness of the water will help to relax and refresh you.

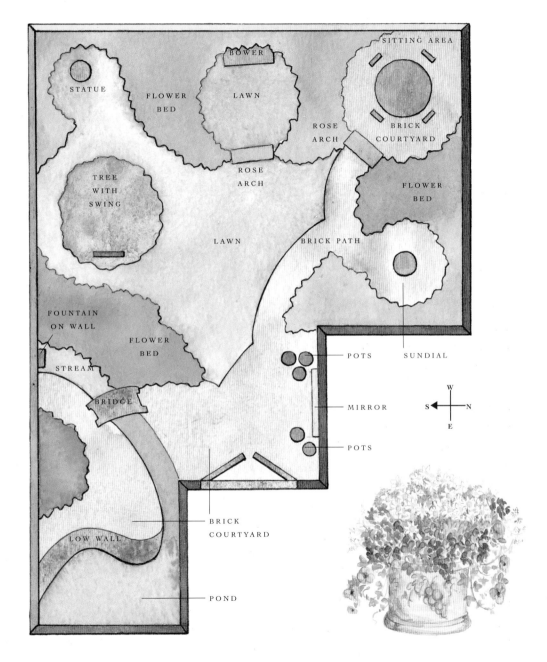

SITTING AREA

STATUE

FLOWER
BED

BOWER

LAWN

ROSE
ARCH

BRICK
COURTYARD

ROSE
ARCH

TREE
WITH
SWING

FLOWER
BED

LAWN

BRICK PATH

FOUNTAIN
ON WALL

FLOWER
BED

STREAM

POTS

SUNDIAL

W
S — N
E

BRIDGE

MIRROR

POTS

BRICK
COURTYARD

LOW WALL

POND

3 Pleasure and indulgence: A large tree stands in this part of the garden, giving cool shade beneath it. A swing has been hung from one of its branches to introduce a little fun and gentle movement into the pleasure and indulgence area. This is the south, yang area of the garden.

4 New beginnings: This is a secluded corner of the garden, with a circle of lawn surrounded by beds of scented flowers. It contains many flowers that smell at their best in the early evening, such as night-scented stock and sweet rocket, as a reminder that early evening can be the beginning of the best part of the day. In the center of the lawn stands a statue of Venus, goddess of love.

5 Relationship: This section of the garden is reached through a rose-covered arch. A circle of grass is surrounded by flowerbeds backed by shrubs that are tall enough to create a private area within. At the back, against the wall, is a bower. A two-seater lovers' bench is surrounded with honeysuckle and jasmine supported on a rustic wooden frame.

left: *Scented plants are full of romance. Lavender gives out its warm odor by day and night-scented stock and nicotiana (not yet in flower) have floating evening odors.*

6 Children and family: This is the area for enjoying company. A circular brick courtyard is just large enough for a table and chairs for sitting out or eating and drinking with friends and family.

7 Wisdom and experience: Here is another private area, this time containing a sundial representing the wisdom and experience that comes with time. It is surrounded by flowerbeds but, except for the shrubs that screen it from the sitting area nearby, most of the plants are low-growing herbs. This is a good area to grow herbs, since herb lore is a very wise and ancient tradition.

8 Wealth: The wealth area is missing from this garden, but this has been remedied by attaching a full-height, arched mirror to the wall of the courtyard. The reflection gives the impression of more garden in the location of the missing wealth section. The mirror is disguised with a trellis frame with evergreen ivy and other climbers growing up it and pots in front of it containing ferns. The mirror reflects the fountain opposite, symbolizing wealth pouring into the area. The bridge is also reflected, adding depth to reinforce the impression that the northeast section is present in the garden.

A Garden for Children

CHILDREN NEED *plenty of stimulation in the garden, and lots of opportunities to explore and use their imagination. A well-designed garden for children provides all of this, and good feng shui will help to insure the children's safety as they play. This garden incorporates all sorts of features for children to enjoy and learn from, both individually and with each other. The garden contains lots of trees, which break up and calm down the yang ch'i from the south-facing entrance.*

The trees provide a sheltered area in which the ch'i flows harmoniously and not too fast, creating a gentle, safe area for children to play. The north part of the garden has been opened up to prevent the north yin ch'i from becoming too sleepy and stagnating. The most heavily wooded part of the garden is in the west, where the trees have a calming effect on the unpredictable west ch'i coming into the garden. The trees are varieties that allow ch'i to flow in and out of the branches easily – mostly beech trees, oak trees, and smaller fruit trees.

This garden would be suitable for children old enough to play safely around water. However, it could easily be adapted for smaller children, keeping the stream very shallow indeed, and perhaps omitting the pool, or maybe fitting it with a metal grille just below the surface so that children cannot fall into it.

The willow tunnel in the garden is made by driving stakes of live willow into the ground to form the outline of the den, and then tying them to meet in an arch

above: Feng shui principles can help to make the children's play area safe as well as enjoyable. The atmosphere should be lively yet calm.

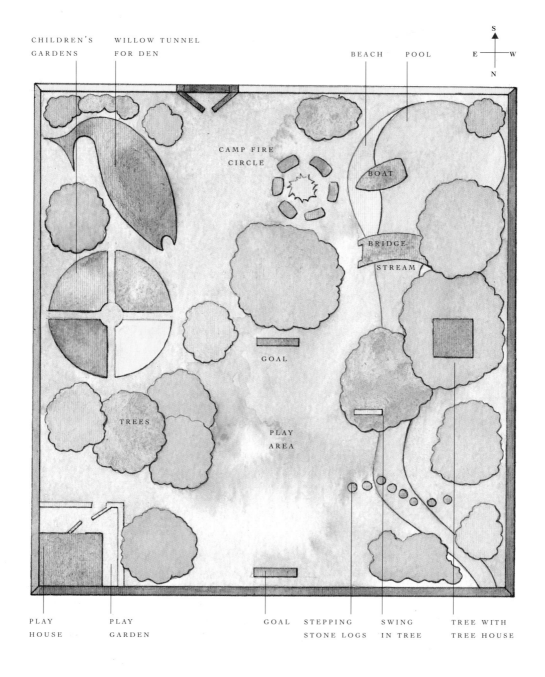

CHILDREN'S
GARDENS

WILLOW TUNNEL
FOR DEN

BEACH   POOL

S

E   W

N

CAMP FIRE
CIRCLE

BOAT

BRIDGE

STREAM

GOAL

TREES

PLAY
AREA

PLAY
HOUSE

PLAY
GARDEN

GOAL

STEPPING
STONE LOGS

SWING
IN TREE

TREE WITH
TREE HOUSE

at the top. Live willow will root and grow when treated like this. As the willow grows, new shoots can be woven in between the original stakes, creating a more solid structure.

THE EIGHT PAH KWA AREAS

1 **Fame:** The entrance is in the south of this garden, and the fame area contains a campfire circle made from logs where children can sit out in the evening cooking campfire meals and telling stories. The campfire acts as a beacon announcing the children's presence and, therefore, fits comfortably into the fame area.

2 **Health and happiness:** This area contains a peaceful pool with a little shingle beach beside it and a small rowboat. An arched bridge crosses the stream where it joins the lake, symbolizing the fact that good health and happiness should bridge every aspect of life.

3 **Pleasure and indulgence:** This wooded area, with the stream flowing through, contains a tree house where the children can let their imagination run wild. The tree house could include poles to slide down, ladders, rope bridges, and anything else to stimulate children. The neighboring tree has a swing hanging from its branches.

4 **New beginnings:** The stream begins in this section of the garden and can be crossed using stepping stones made of logs placed on their ends.

5 **Relationship:** This part of the garden has been cleared to make way for an open games area, with soccer goals at either end of it. In order to play games such as football, the children have to learn to work together in teams.

6 **Children and family:** This is the place to learn to play house, and this corner of the garden contains a playhouse with its own little garden, enclosed by a picket fence.

7 **Wisdom and experience:** A circular flowerbed has been created here for children to learn about gardening. The flowerbed is divided into sections, one for each child.

8 **Wealth:** A giant fish, representing wealth, has been created out of woven willow branches, making a den that is open at both ends – the head and the tail – like a tunnel. The willow is still growing, which suits the southeast area of the garden, where life remedies are at their most effective.

right: Planting tall-growing flowers to give color and dappled shade has a salutary softening effect on a children's sandpit and makes a peaceful play area.

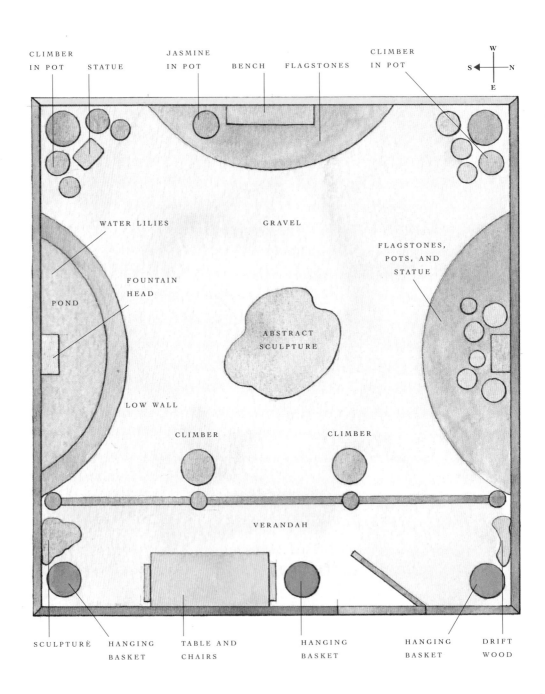

CLIMBER IN POT   STATUE   JASMINE IN POT   BENCH   FLAGSTONES   CLIMBER IN POT

W N S E

WATER LILIES

GRAVEL

FOUNTAIN HEAD

FLAGSTONES, POTS, AND STATUE

POND

ABSTRACT SCULPTURE

LOW WALL

CLIMBER   CLIMBER

VERANDAH

SCULPTURE   HANGING BASKET   TABLE AND CHAIRS   HANGING BASKET   HANGING BASKET   DRIFT WOOD

A Courtyard Garden

MANY TOWN HOUSES *have only small gardens, walled or fenced all around, with access only from the house. These gardens are often too small to have room for any lawn and have only limited space for sitting out or for growing plants. However, Chinese houses are often constructed around a central courtyard, and this kind of garden is traditionally thought to have excellent feng shui potential. The garden on these pages can only be entered from the house on the east side and is surrounded by high walls.*

Ch'i hates clutter – it inhibits its movement – so one of the most important things you can do with a small garden is to keep it clear and tidy so that the ch'i can flow. Fix that broken bit of trellis, give the backdoor a fresh coat of paint, clear away any garbage or mess, and choose attractive flower pots for your plants.

It isn't necessary for every garden to contain elements suitable for each of the eight pah kwa areas; but it is important that none of the areas contain anything unsuitable, such as a bonfire in the money area (unless you have money to burn). Good feng shui that encourages ch'i to flow harmoniously is all that is needed.

In a small garden such as this you would normally expect only a few features, which should be placed appropriately.

There is little room for flowerbeds, so all the plants are in pots. The walls of this courtyard are quite high, so they have been softened with climbers planted in pots in the corners. A glass-covered veranda has been created against the wall of the house so it is possible to sit out even if the weather is wet.

The courtyard is graveled with flagstones set into it in places. In the center of the garden is an abstract piece of sculpture with a hole running horizontally through it, which helps the ch'i to circulate.

THE EIGHT PAH KWA AREAS

1 Fame: The backdoor opens onto the flagstoned veranda area, which can be used for entertaining whatever the weather. Since this is in the east, where the element of wood is at home, the veranda is supported on wooden posts.

2 Health and happiness: The table and chairs are sited in the area of health and happiness. In the corner behind them is a hanging basket, which encourages the ch'i to flow around the corner where the house meets the garden rather than becoming trapped under the back corner of the veranda. The end wall of the veranda also contains an abstract modern sculpture of curving shapes.

3 Pleasure and indulgence: There is a pond here, fed by a fountainhead on the wall in the shape of a head, with the water spouting from its mouth. The edge of the pond is raised for sitting on.

4 New beginnings: In the corner of the garden is a statue surrounded by pots of plants, many of them evergreen, including a pot from which a climber grows to cover the walls.

above: *Climbers and plants in raised beds surrounding an uncluttered central area are excellent feng shui.*

5 Relationship: In this part of the garden a bench sits on a semicircle of flagstones. The bench is made of metal, the element that belongs in the west of the garden. A scented jasmine climbs up the wall behind it.

6 Children and family: A group of potted plants softens this corner, and a climber grows up the wall on trellis.

7 Wisdom and experience: This side of the garden features a statue of Athena, goddess of wisdom, on a plinth. The walls behind are covered with ivy.

8 Wealth: This corner has a hanging basket to keep the ch'i moving. The end wall of the veranda also has a large piece of driftwood. It is a reminder, in the wealth area, that good fortune can be found unexpectedly and does not always have to be worked for.

left: *Even a small town garden can have a summerhouse in a sunny area. Trelliswork makes a boundary which opens up the garden while giving it a sense of containment.*

A Zen Garden

JAPANESE ZEN GARDENS, *although the product of a culture different from the one that developed the principles of feng shui, nevertheless contain ancient links with the art of feng shui. Certainly it is hard to find a good example of a Zen garden that does not also have good feng shui. Such gardens are peaceful and meditative, allowing the ch'i to circulate gently, and have a pleasant balance of light and shade. This east-facing garden is designed to occupy a relatively small space; you don't need a lot of room to create a Zen garden.*

Many people associate Zen gardens with vast expanses of raked gravel and stones. These are known as "dry gardens"; the gravel represents water and yin, and the stones represent land and yang. But they are not the only kind of Zen garden. While they tend to have very good feng shui, ch'i is happiest in a garden with more life and greenery, and with real water. The Zen garden shown here is still very simple and designed for meditation.

The garden has a pool at its center surrounded by moss and ferns. The pool

left: *A Zen garden can be created in the smallest area and always provides a place for contemplation.*

opposite: *While Zen gardens can be an austere combination of raked gravel and stones, living plants can be a welcome addition.*

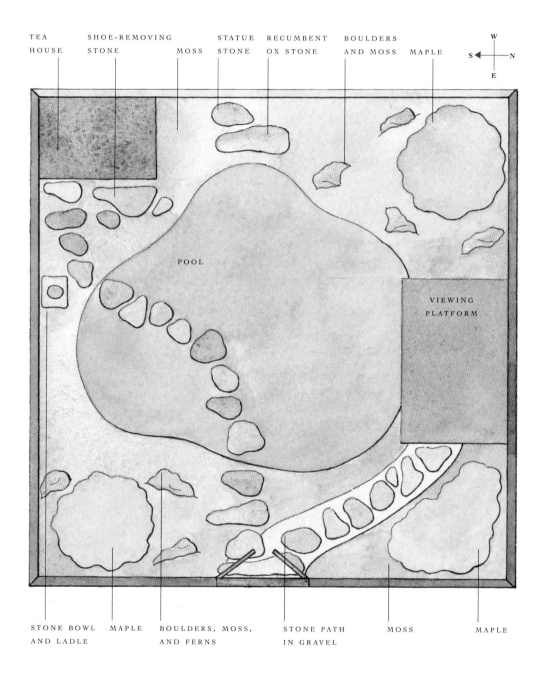

TEA
HOUSE

SHOE-REMOVING
STONE

MOSS

STATUE
STONE

RECUMBENT
OX STONE

BOULDERS
AND MOSS

MAPLE

W
S ← → N
E

POOL

VIEWING
PLATFORM

STONE BOWL
AND LADLE

MAPLE

BOULDERS, MOSS,
AND FERNS

STONE PATH
IN GRAVEL

MOSS

MAPLE

is very shallow, and the bottom is covered with cobblestones, which can be seen clearly through the water. It contains no fish and moves only with the breeze rippling the surface. The fence around the garden is made of upright bamboo posts.

On the west side of the garden stand two large rocks. Rocks are an essential feature of Zen gardens – they are yang while water is yin – and each is believed to have its own character. The more signs of age, such as erosion and lichen, the better the boulder is considered to be. Certain rock shapes are thought to be especially beneficial to meditation.

THE EIGHT PAH KWA AREAS

1 Fame: The doorway from the house into the garden is in the east, and there is a choice of paths. This area of the garden is open and spacious.

2 Health and happiness: In this corner of the garden, moss and ferns grow in between ancient boulders covered with lichen.

3 Pleasure and indulgence: The stepping stone path across the pool bends toward this part of the garden. The ground at the edge of the pool is covered with moss, and the bamboo fence is visible behind it.

4 New beginnings: Outside the tea house it is a stone bowl with a ladle to wash hands and mouths so that one enters the tea house renewed and purified. There is also a shoe-removing stone to leave one's shoes on while inside. The entrance to the tea house is low so that it is necessary to humble oneself by stooping or crawling to enter it. This tea house has a circular entrance and incorporates openwork bamboo screens so that the ch'i can flow in and out.

5 Relationship: This area contains a statue stone – a tall stone – behind a long, low boulder, higher at one end than the other, known as a recumbent ox stone. The juxtaposition of these two stones represents a perfect relationship of different principles in balance.

6 Children and family: In this part of the garden a maple tree stands behind a landscape of moss-covered boulders.

7 Wisdom and experience: Here is a viewing platform, projecting a little over the edge of the pool, made of slatted wood. It is an ideal position from which to contemplate the garden.

8 Wealth: This area is covered with moss with a path of stepping stones set into gravel leading from the door to the viewing platform.

Index

PICTURE ACKNOWLEDGMENTS

Cover: Clive Nichols
Courtesy of Tony & Glen Eastman: 32, 34 (with Philip
Booth), 69 *right*, 72, 73; **Garden Matters:** 18, 49, 74, 77;
Garden Picture Library: 8–9 (Steven Wooster), 15
(Brigitte Thomas), 19 (Nick Meers), 24 (Steven Wooster),
30 (Ron Sutherland), 39 (Brigitte Thomas), 45
(Lamontagne), 54 (Jerry Pavia), 59 (Juliette Wade), 63
(J S Sira), 64 (Ron Sutherland), 65 (Steven Wooster), 82
(Sunniva Harte), 88 (Brigitte Thomas), 97 (Marijke Heuff);
Jerry Harpur: 11, 43 (Designer: Julie Toll), 66 (Designer:
Bobbi Hicks), 81, 101 (Designer: Keelya Meadows);
Andrew Lawson: 47, 50, 53, 60, 61, 71, 75; **courtesy of
Liz McGowan:** 69 *left*, 73 *right*; **Clive Nichols:** 12 (Mr
Fraser/J Teyer-Evans), 27 (Designer: Dan Pearson), 33
(Designer: Paula Rainey-Crofts), 46 (Designer: Julie Toll),
56 (Designer: Julie Toll), 94, 100, 102, 103; **Hugh Palmer:**
23, 29, 37, 41, 55, 68, 78, 79, 92